ERRAIN

WRITING THE TERRAIN

TRAVELLING THROUGH ALBERTA WITH THE POETS

EDITED BY ROBERT M. STAMP

UNIVERSITY OF
CALGARY
PRESS

© 2005 by Robert M. Stamp

Published by the
University of Calgary Press
2500 University Drive NW
Calgary, Alberta, Canada T2N 1N4
www.uofcpress.com

We acknowledge the financial
support of the Government of Canada
through the Book Publishing Industry
Development Program (BPIDP), the
Alberta Foundation for the Arts and
the Alberta Lottery Fund—Community
Initiatives Program for our publishing
activities. We acknowledge the support
of the Canada Council for the Arts for
our publishing program.

Canada Council   Conseil des Arts
for the Arts   du Canada

Canadä

ALBERTA
LOTTERY FUND

LIBRARY AND ARCHIVES OF CANADA
CATALOGUING IN PUBLICATION:

Writing the terrain : travellling through
Alberta with the poets / edited by
Robert M. Stamp.

Poems.

ISBN   1-55238-136-6

1   Alberta–Poetry.
2   Landscape–Poetry.
3   Canadian poetry
    (English)–20th century.
4   Canadian poetry (English)–
    21st century.
I   Stamp, Robert M., 1937–

PS8295.5.A4W75 2005
C811'.54080327123
C2005-900992-6

Cover photos by John Dean.
Cover design by Mieka West.
Internal design & typesetting
    by Jason Dewinetz.

∞   This book is printed on
Rolland Enviro Edition Natural,
a 100% post-consumer paper.
Printed and bound in Canada by
HIGNELL PRINTING.

xi   INTRODUCTION

1 WRITING THE PROVINCE

1   Barry McKinnon, *untitled*
3   Dennis Cooley, *labiarinth*
4   Joan Shillington, *I Was Born Alberta*
5   Nancy Holmes, *The Right Frame of Mind*
6   George Bowering, *it's the climate*
7   Charles Noble, *Mnemonic Without Portfolio*
8   John O. Thompson, *Fuel Crisis*
9   Robert Stamp, *Energy to Burn*

2 WRITING CALGARY

13   Ian Adam, *In Calgary These Things*
14   George Bowering, *calgary*
15   Murdoch Burnett, *Boys or the River*
17   Anne Campbell, *Calgary City Wind*
18   Weyman Chan, *Written on Water*
19   Ryan Fitzpatrick, *From the Ogden Shops*
21   Cecelia Frey, *Under the Louise Bridge*
22   Gail Ghai, *On a Winter Hill Overlooking Calgary*
23   Deborah Godin, *Time/Lapse Calgary as Bremen*
24   Vivian Hansen, *Wolf Willow against the bridge*
25   Robert Hilles, *When Light Transforms Flesh*
26   Nancy Holmes, *Calgary Mirage*
27   Bruce Hunter, *Wishbone*
28   Pauline Johnson, *Calgary of the Plains*
29   Robert Kroetsch, *Horsetail Sonnet*
30   Erin Michie, *The Willows at Weaselhead*
31   Deborah Miller, *Pictures from the Stampede*
33   James M. Moir, *This City by the Bow*
34   Colin Morton, *Calgary '80*
36   Erin Mouré, *South-West, or Altadore*
40   Roberta Rees, *Because Calgary*
41   Robert Stamp, *A City Built for Speed*

42   Yvonne Trainer, *1912*

43   Aritha van Herk, *Quadrant Four – Outskirts of Outskirts*

48   Wilfred Watson, *In the Cemetery of the Sun*

50   Christopher Wiseman, *Calgary 2 A.M.*

51   Rita Wong, *Sunset Grocery*

3   WRITING SOUTHWESTERN ALBERTA & THE FOOTHILLS

55   D.C. Reid, *Drying Out Again*

56   Ian Adam, *The Big Rocks*

57   George Bowering, *high river alberta*

58   Cecelia Frey, *Woman in a potato field north of Nanton*

60   Sheri-D Wilson, *He Went by Joe*

62   Charles Noble, *Props64*

63   Stacie Wolfer, *Lethbridge*

65   Karen Solie, *Java Shop, Fort Macleod*

66   Sid Marty, *Death Song for the Oldman*

67   Michael Cullen, *wind down waterton lakes*

68   Ian Adam, *Job Description*

70   Jan Boydol, *Color Hillcrest Dead*

71   Aislinn Hunter, *Frank Slide, Alberta*

72   r. rickey, *this way crowsnest*

74   Ken Rivard, *Turner Valley*

75   Allan Serafino, *Hay Rolls Near Millarville*

76   Miriam Waddington, *Mountain Interval II*

4   WRITING SOUTHEASTERN ALBERTA & THE BADLANDS

83   Joan Crate, *Gleichen*

84   Walter Hildebrandt, *Brooks Aqueduct*

85   John Barton, *This Side of the Border*

86   Tim Lilburn, *Now, Lifted, Now*

87   Jan Zwicky, *Highway 879*

88   Monty Reid, *Writing-on-Stone*

89   Tim Lilburn, *Kill-site*

90   Yvonne Trainer, *What can Anybody See?*

91   Sid Marty, *Medicine Hat*

93   Karen Solie, *Suffield*

94   Monty Reid, *Bonebed: Dinosaur Provincial Park*

95   Kim Maltman, *Ice Fishing Cessford Lake*

96   Tim Bowling, *Midday, Midsummer*

97   Cecelia Frey, *Wind at Oyen, alta.*

98   Richard Woollatt, *Highway 9, East of Hanna*

99   Jason Dewinetz, *Badlands*

101   Christine Wiesenthal, *Avian specimen*

103   Bruce Hunter, *Slow Learner*

5   WRITING THE BOW CORRIDOR: CALGARY TO BANFF

107   Tom Henihan, *Bow Valley*

108   Rajinderpal Pal, *trust*

109   Erin Mouré, *Seebe*

111   Kim Maltman, *Yamnuska*

113   Rosalee van Stelten, *The Three Sisters*

114   Robert Hilles, *Progress*

116   Colin Morton, *at bankhead*

117   Ian Adam, *Trip to Banff*

119   Margaret Avison, *Banff*

120   Gordon Burles, *Reunion*

122   Cyril Dabydeen, *By Lake Minnewanka*

124   Lorne Daniel, *Winter at the Banff School*

126   Richard Hornsey, *The Rocky Mountain Summer Movie*

128   William Latta, *Heat Near Banff*

129   Sid Marty, *The Sand Pile*

130   Erin Mouré, *Cardiac Grizzlies*

131   Charles Noble, *Banff: Space / Time Swindle*

133   Ruth Roach Pierson, *Up Tunnel Mountain Trail*

134   Christopher Wiseman, *In the Banff Springs Hotel*

6   WRITING THE MOUNTAINS: BANFF TO JASPER

139   Fiona Lam, *Departure (Highway to Lake Louise)*

140   Jim Green, *Power Line to Sunshine*

141   Vanna Tessier, *Stone Jack*

142   Jon Whyte, *Wenkchemna*

143   Jon Whyte, *Mind Over Mountains*

144   Carol Ann Sokoloff, *Great Divide*

145   Tammy Armstrong, *Columbia Ice Field*

146   Sid Marty, *Saskatchewan Crossing Café*

147   Douglas Barbour, *in Maligne Canyon*

152   David McFadden, *Mountain Air*

155   Doug Beardsley, *Jasper Bears*

156   Tom Wayman, *A Reason*

158   Sid Marty, *Yellowhead*

7 WRITING THE WESTERN PARKLANDS

163   Rosalee van Stelten, *Didsbury Auction*

165   Tim Bowling, *Cemetery at Olds*

166   Alice Major, *Near Red Deer*

167   Stephan Stephansson, *My Region*

168   Lorne Daniel, *Season of Leaving*

170   Bruce Hunter, *Meditations on the Improbable History of a Small Town*

172   Gerald Hill, *Sisters of the Garden*

173   Ken Rivard, *Gull Lake Alphabet*

174   Monty Reid, *The Alumni Game at Lacombe Arena*

175   Sally Ito, *At the Reynolds Museum, Wetaskiwin, Alberta*

176   John O. Thompson, *Coal Lake*

179   Erin Mouré, *Westerose*

8 WRITING THE EASTERN PARKLANDS

185   Richard Woollatt, *North of Three Hills, the Parklands Begin*

187   Bonnie Bishop, *The Rumsey Moraine*

188   Richard Woollatt, *North & West*

190   Alice Major, *South of Stettler*

191   Richard Woollatt, *Roads to Buffalo Lake*

193   Robert Kroetsch, *Seed Catalogue*

196   Bruce Hunter, *For My Brother Daniel*

197   Tim Lilburn, *Hearing*

198   Alexa DeWiel, *Two Hills*

199   Monty Reid, *The Road Back and Forth to Ryley*

201   Anna Mioduchowska, *Tawayik Lake on the First Sunday in March*

9 WRITING EDMONTON

205   Douglas Barbour, *Edmonton October Poem*

206   Tim Bowling, *A Cup of Coffee in Solitude*

208   Leonard Cohen, *Edmonton, Alberta, December 1966, 4 a.m.*

209   Lorne Daniel, *Fort Edmonton Park*

210   Cecelia Frey, *The Old Edmonton Public Library*

212   Gary Geddes, *Last Tango in Edmonton*

213   Leslie Greentree, *Fargo's, Whyte Avenue*

214   Gerald Hill, *On Line*

215 Laurence Hutchman, *Record Cold*
216 Alice Major, *Persephone on 129 Street*
218 Eli Mandel, *Edmonton's Streets Are Numbered*
220 Miriam Mandel, *Edmonton, May 23, 1978*
222 Erin Mouré, *alta, granite marble & stone co. edmonton*
223 P.K. Page, *Skyline*
224 Joseph Pivato, *Edmonton S.P.Q.R.*
225 Stephen Scobie, *February Edmonton*
226 Peter Stevens, *November Edmonton*
227 Ivan Sundal, *Edmonton, 2000, Summer*
228 Anne Swannell, *At the Ice Palace*
231 John O. Thompson, *Stucco'd (Edmonton-*
232 James Thurgood, *smash the window*
235 Phyllis Webb, *Edmonton Centre, Sept. 23/80*

10 WRITING NORTHEASTERN ALBERTA & THE BOREAL FORESTS

239 Tom Wayman, *Highway 2 North of Edmonton, Alberta*
240 E.D. Blodgett, *margins of Morinville*
241 Stephen Scobie, *Songs on the Radio*
243 E.D. Blodgett, *Returning to Busby, Alta.*
244 Robert Boates, *Late September*
245 Richard Hornsey, *Testing the Spring Run*
246 Monty Reid, *73L 23 2 79*
247 Stephen Scobie, *On the Road to Bonnyville*
248 Colleen Thibaudeau, *All My Nephews Have Gone to the Tar Sands*
249 Eva Tihanyi, *Elk Lake Imperative*
250 Tim Bowling, *Final Night in Fort Chipewyan*

11 WRITING NORTHWESTERN ALBERTA & THE PEACE RIVER COUNTRY

255 Eli Mandel, *Wabamun*
258 Michael Henry, *Pilgrimage to Lac Ste. Anne*
259 Jan Zwicky, *Passing Sangudo*
261 Rajinderpal Pal, *solstice*
262 Greg Simison, *Grouard Cemetery*
263 Erin Mouré, *Grande Prairie: So Far From Poland*
264 Tom Howe, *Prosser's House*
266 James Wreford Watson, *The Northlands, Peace River: Alta.*
269 Aleksei Kazuk, *Walking Into the Mandala: Fort Vermillion*
270 Miriam Waddington, *Waiting in Alberta*

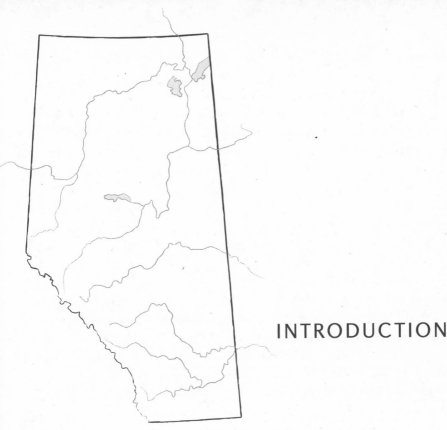

INTRODUCTION

What is the relationship between poems written in and about Canada and the Canadian landscape? D.M.R. Bentley poses this question in introducing *The Gay/Grey Moose: Essays on the Ecologies and Mythologies of Canadian Poetry* (1992). Bentley is neither the first nor the latest critic to explore this link between writing and the land. Canadian literature takes for granted that landscape is a legitimate subject. "We have assumed that engagement with the land is a subject of intense interest and depictions of its grandeur, immensity and variety a primary source of aesthetic pleasure," asserts Susan Glickman in *The Picturesque & the Sublime: A Poetics of the Canadian Landscape* (1988). This seems especially true in poetry, concludes Tom Marshall in *Harsh and Lonely Land* (1979), since "all Canadian poets past and present from all parts of the country have been obsessed with wilderness and space."

This preoccupation with place is most evident in the poetry of the Canadian prairies. In his introduction to *Twelve Prairie Poets* (1976), Laurence Ricou argues that "the prairie is a prominent, and often persistent, focus of the poet's work." Place also dominates Birk Sproxton's edited collection, *Trace: Prairie Writers on Writing* (1986), where poet Anne Szumigalski maintains that "this prairie, this place to which we have come, or from which we have emerged, has never so far failed in its overriding influence on those who write in it and of it." In the 1997 edition of *The Oxford Companion to Canadian Literature,* Cynthia Messenger asserts that the "evocation of place continues to be a strength in Canadian poetry," using Robert Kroetsch's *Excerpts from the Real World* (1986), with its references to Outlook, Saskatchewan, and Riding Mountain, Manitoba as "splendid example[s] of how the Canadian landscape, particularly the prairie, can find its way into love poetry."

Geographers have also joined this poetry/place discussion. For the past generation, literature has been espoused by a growing band of geographers seeking alternative perspectives and insights in the study of man/environmental relationships. "Disillusioned by an era of logical positivism, maybe shell-shocked by the quantitative revolution, perhaps rediscovering the literary heritage of geography," Douglas Pocock writes in *Humanistic Geography and Literature* (1981), the "realm of literature has attracted increasing attention from our eclectic discipline." Literary creations, argue Allen Noble and Ramesh Dhussa in "Image and Substance" (*Journal of Cultural Geography,* 1990), offer geographers "valuable and sometimes unique types of information conveying feelings, viewpoints, values, attitudes, and meanings associated with landscape and place." Literary works might be viewed as "data banks consisting of subtle and elusive bits of information stored by sensitive, perceptive, and imaginative writers, who may respond to stimuli and landscapes in a different fashion than academically trained geographers.

But what is place? In *RePlacing: Essays on Canadian Writing* (1980), Dennis Cooley emphasizes the *voice* of place, with prairie poets writing "out of an increasingly vernacular voice found in the people and events around them." In his oft-cited article, "Writing West" (*Canadian Forum,* 1977), Eli Mandel offers his image for the prairie writer as "one who returns," that is, as "a man [woman] not so much in place, as one out of place and so one endlessly trying to get back, to find his [her] way home, to return, to write himself [herself] into existence, writing west." The place that interests Mandel is a state of mind, "a tension between place and culture, a doubleness or duplicity," a state that is grounded not in "nostalgia, sadness, memory, even affection" of place, but in language and form. Echoing Mandel, historian Douglas Francis maintains in *Images of the West* (1980), that in the post-World War II era, "the prairies have been transformed into a state of mind." Ceasing to be associated directly with a physical locale, the "image of the West is of a landscape of the mind, moulded by the myths and realities of a western Canadian tradition." For Francis, there continues to be a "healthy and creative tension between perception of image and reality."

Despite these world views of literary critics and cultural geographers, place in prairie and Alberta literature and poetry was traditionally presented as narrowly and essentially rural – and a rural community engaged primarily in farming and ranching. "When one turns to the open prairies, the cities and towns fade into the background and life concerns itself with the fortunes of the elements," asserted James Wreford Watson in "Canadian Regionalism in Life and Letters" (*The Geographical Journal*, 1965). This is not only due to "few cities and consequently, a far greater stretch of sky," but also because the skies "hold the promise of help or threat of disaster to the Prairie dweller," who lives "on a knife-edge of hope between the despairs of frost and the terrors of drought."

Older Alberta literary anthologies support this orientation. W.G. Hardy's *The Alberta Golden Jubilee Anthology* (1955) presented a province essentially rural in its landscape and mindset. His Alberta was characterized by "the vastness of its territory … the variety of its scenery from prairie to foothill to mountain and lake and muskeg and forest." Even when Hardy looked to Alberta's future, with "a polyglot of peoples" flourishing in a "Land of Opportunity," his rural landscape continued to dominate, "from the rolling prairies of the south to the permafrost of the Precambrian Shield that slices across its northern portions." This rural emphasis persisted. Neither John Patrick Gillese's *Chinook Arch: A Centennial Anthology of Alberta Writing* (1967) nor John Chalmers' *Alberta Diamond Jubilee Anthology* (1980) addressed Alberta's growing urbanization. Pamela Banting's *Fresh Tracks* (1998) is a more recent anthology of new western Canadian writing that explores the "ways in which we both imprint and are imprinted by geography." While the book is certainly "about writing the land," Banting's predominant interest lies in "the environment, nature writing and sense of place." The defined landscape remains rural.

Only slowly have editors and critics acknowledged an urban dimension to prairie writing. In *The Prairie Experience* (1975), Terry Angus grudgingly admits that a "characteristic motif of prairie writing is the rural-to-urban shift, the leaving of the land for the city" with that literature often contrasting the "mores and the moral implications of rural and urban life." Yet Angus stands firmly for the rural: "The farmer, however, remains the symbol of the prairies. He seems to stand for the common man, for the moral fibre of the west. Without him the west would be the east." In *Glass Canyons: A Collection of Calgary Fiction and Poetry* (1985), Ian Adam suggests that the failure of Alberta's cityscapes to penetrate these early anthologies may be in part due to the transiency of the city versus the permanency of the rural landscape.

"Calgary seems to be under erasure," Adam notes. "It would rather always be transforming itself than settle for a stable identity." He concludes that "any definitive statement about Calgary has to be provisional," for "it would be out of the city's character to be otherwise."

Laurie Ricou was one of the first to note a broadening focus of prairie poetry. "The land itself is a less prominent subject than one might suppose," he wrote in "Poems of the Prairie" (*NeWest Review,* 1975) "The people and the memories are catching more and more of the poet's attention." Four years later, in "The Three Provinces of Prairie Poetry" (*NeWest Review,* 1979), Ricou again addressed the diversity of subject matter beginning to challenge the "wind and dust tradition" of prairie poetry. "A more urban poetry, a poetry turned less toward the land than to manners and society," seems inevitable. Several recent Alberta literary anthologies acknowledge this new order, especially Aritha van Herk's *Alberta Rebound* (1990) and *Boundless Alberta* (1993) and Fred Stenson's *The Road Home: New Stories from Alberta Writers* (1992). "Stand at any busy intersection for ten minutes and you can see what Alberta is," observes Stenson in his introduction. Or, as editor Srdja Pavlovic remarks in *Threshold: An Anthology of Contemporary Writing from Alberta* (1999), this province's writers offer "tools for analyzing urban living."

This rural-to-urban shift in both population and cultural concerns is featured in *Writing the Terrain: Travelling through Alberta with the Poets.* We begin with Barry McKinnon's "untitled" piece, which asks the question "do you expect poems / of giant grain elevators / and miles / of golden wheat." Farmer-poet Charles Noble is well aware that the province's farming population has dropped from over 50 per cent in the early twentieth century to less than 5 per cent today. His "Props" celebrates the joys and hardships of working a 135-acre field of spring wheat on his family's land near Nobleford, while his "Mnemonic Without Portfolio" captures the rural-to-urban shift in Alberta's population and its writing. The final line of "Mnemonic Without Portfolio" – "they changed the rural/urban representation" – is a poetic punchline to a rather enigmatic poem.

Yet much of the critically acclaimed poetry that addresses Alberta major cities presents a dismal picture of urban life. This bleakness is also evident in George Bowering's "The Streets of Calgary" and Aritha van Herk's "Calgary, this growing graveyard." Or consider the poetic portrayal of Edmonton as a city of snow, cold, and seemingly perpetual winter, as in Leonard Cohen's "Edmonton, Alberta." Early representative anthologies of both Calgary and Edmonton writing do little to brighten this gloom. By their very titles, *Glass Canyons: A Collection of Calgary Fiction and Poetry* (1985) and *39 Below: The Anthology of Contemporary Edmonton Poetry* (1973) suggest cities of chilling coldness, whether the frigidity be climatic or commercial.

Beyond the major cities, successive waves of people – and poetry – have continually challenged and contested the nature of land and landscape. First Nations poets, pioneer European poets, contemporary poets from every continent who have chosen to live and write in Alberta – all interpret the land differently. While the unspoiled land as pure agricultural resource infuses Noble's poetry, *Writing the Terrain* includes poems revealing a landscape altered by technology: Walter Hildebrandt's "Brooks Aqueduct" and Karen Solie's "Suffield." Meanwhile, the mining industry is represented in Jan Boydol's "Color Hillcrest Dead," Aislinn Hunter's "Frank Slide, Alberta," and Colin Morton's "at bankhead;" while the petroleum industry surfaces in John O. Thompson's "Fuel Crisis," Bob Stamp's "Energy to Burn," Ken Rivard's "Turner Valley," and Colleen Thibaudeau's "All My Nephews Have Gone to the Tar Sands."

§

Writing the Terrain: Travelling through Alberta with the Poets spotlights both the multitudinous assaults on Alberta's landscape and the rural-to-urban population shift. By including poems of city and country, prairie and parkland, mountain and valley, *Writing the Terrain* reflects the diversity of the province's multi-landscaped geography. By featuring writers whose responses to provincial sites range from abject despair to exaltation, *Writing Alberta* reflects not just a variety of specific poets' feelings but the complicated nature of the human condition in all its forms.

What qualifies as "Alberta" poetry? *Writing the Terrain* follows in the expansive tradition of Ricou's *Twelve Prairie Poets* (1976), which sought poems that showed the "quality and variety of prairie poetry," especially "poems that both create and depend upon a sense of the locale and history" of the Canadian prairie. "Whether these poems are accurate pictures of places or people is not especially relevant" to Ricou. Rather, the "fertile questions are how the poet has created the region through language, and what details of the region he has used to reveal the universal." And what makes a poet an "Alberta" poet? *Writing the Terrain* avoids narrow rules about length of residency or "commitment" to the province. Like Daniel Lenoski's *a/long prairie lines: An Anthology of Long Prairie Poems* (1989), our choices are determined "by a literary corpus that operate[s] as explorer, archaeologist, namer, traveller and actor" in order to "cover as many western constituencies as possible – generic, geographical, historical, ethnic, rural, urban, and domestic."

George Bowering is well represented in *Writing the Terrain*. Canada's first poet laureate spent only two brief years here in the early 1960s – teaching English at the University of Alberta at Calgary (now the University of Calgary) before returning to his native British Columbia. Yet Bowering's unflattering poetic response to the province ("it's the climate"), to Calgary ("calgary"), and to the foothills country ("high river, alberta"), were all included in *Rocky Mountain Foot* (1968), which earned him the Governor General's Award for Poetry. Bowering is but one of a long list of Governor General's poetry award winners in *Writing the Terrain*. Many are career-long Alberta writers, such as Robert Kroetsch ("Horsetail Sonnet" and "Seed Catalogue"), Robert Hilles ("When Light Transforms Flesh"), and Edmonton's E.D. Blodgett ("margins of Morinville"). Other Governor General's winners spent early parts of their career in this province before moving on – Erin Mouré ("South-West, or Altadore"), Eli Mandel ("Edmonton's Streets are Numbered"), Stephen Scobie ("February Edmonton"). While many of the GG's included in *Writing the Terrain* seem merely to have passed through, nevertheless the provincial landscape impressed them. Consider Wilfred Watson ("In the Cemetery of the Sun"), Jan Zwicky ("Highway 879"), Margaret Avison ("Banff"), Tom Wayman ("A Reason"), Leonard Cohen ("Edmonton, Alberta, December 1966"), P.K. Page ("Skyline"), all the way back to James Wreford Watson ("From the Place on the Map") winner of the Governor General's Medal for Poetry in 1950.

Writing the Terrain includes other established poets. Like Charles Noble, many are closely associated with the provincial literary scene: Jon Whyte ("Mind Over Mountains"), Ian Adam ("In Calgary These Things"), Aritha van Herk ("Quadrant Four – Outskirts of Outskirts"), Cecelia Frey ("Under the Louise Bridge"), Vivian Hansen ("Wolf Willow against the Bridge"), Christopher Wiseman ("Calgary 2 A.M."), Sheri-D Wilson ("He Went by Joe"), Sid Marty ("Death Song for the Oldman"), Ken Rivard ("Turner Valley"), Tim Bowling ("Midday, Midsummer"), Douglas Barbour ("in Maligne Canyon"), Monty Reid ("Bonebed: Dinosaur Provincial Park"), and Tom Henihan ("Bow Valley"). Still, poets from outside the province have shown themselves equally capable of thoughtful responses to the Alberta landscape: Dennis Cooley ("labiarinth"), Miriam Waddington ("Waiting in Alberta"), Cyril Dabydeen ("By Lake Minnewanka"), David McFadden ("Mountain Air"), Tim Lilburn ("Now, Lifted, Now"), and Peter Stevens ("November Edmonton").

Writing the Terrain also features emerging poets, including Rajinderpal Pal ("trust" and "solstice"), Rita Wong ("sunset grocery"), Joan Crate ("Gleichen"), Sally Ito ("At the Reynolds Museum, Wetaskiwin"), Weyman Chan ("Written on Water"), Leslie Greentree ("Fargo's, Whyte Avenue"), Ryan Fitzpatrick ("from the ogden shops"), Erin Michie ("The Willows at Weaselhead"), Karen Solie ("Java Shop, Fort Macleod"), Aislinn Hunter ("Frank Slide, Alberta"), Jason Dewinetz ("Badlands"), Rosalee van Stelten ("The Three Sisters"), Fiona Lam ("Departure"), Vanna Tessier ("Stone Jack"), Tammy Armstrong ("Columbia Ice Field"), Ivan Sundal ("Edmonton, 2000, Summer"), and Joan Shillington ("I Was Born Alberta").

Writing the Terrain is the first anthology dedicated solely to poetry of the Alberta landscape – to its townscapes and cityscapes in addition to its rural areas. It offers a series of poetic journeys through Calgary and Edmonton, through the southwestern foothills, badlands and mountains, parklands and northern boreal forests. This collection of poetry is not sanctioned by Travel Alberta; nor is it likely to be featured by local tourist bureaus and chambers of commerce. *Writing the Terrain* presents a very different view of Alberta than that touted by tour operators. Here, we feature a series of journeys through the province with poets as our guides.

Yet poems selected for *Writing the Terrain* go beyond mere "place-poetry." As Edward Field argues in his introduction to an American collection entitled *A New Geography of Poets* (1992), "it is not our interest to settle for mere landscape poetry but to choose poems that reveal the spirit of the place and of the poet, aiming for a balance between inner and outer geography." A place may inspire, argues Leonard Lutwack in *The Role of Place in Literature* (1984), but a "balance must be maintained between the place that inspires and the poet who is inspired, between object and subject." Some questions readers might ask of landscape poetry: Does the poet respond to landscape rather than merely observing it? Does the poet feel the landscape in addition to seeing it? Does the poet reflect upon landscape's effect upon the mind? Does the poet transcend the limitations of logical, visual or geographic space in order to bring into existence a poetry of multiple elements in fluid intimacy?

§

My interest in the relationship between poetry and place began more than twenty years ago, when I coordinated the interdisciplinary Canadian Studies Program at the University of Calgary. That initial interest was sparked in part by the late James Wreford Watson, a geographer from Edinburgh University who twice taught in the program as a visiting professor. Watson, with a distinguished career in both Canada and Great Britain, won the Governor General's Medal with his 1950 poetry collection, *Of Time and the Lover,* and helped pioneer the field of cultural geography. My nascent interest in culture and landscape led to a short article, "Where Does Geography End and Literature Begin?" (*The Operational Geographer,* 1983) and influenced my entry on Alberta in the 1985 edition of *The Canadian Encyclopedia.* Though I left the field of Canadian Studies for various careers both within and without academia, I am forever indebted to Wreford Watson for the skill he demonstrated in marrying his poetic talent with his academic training in geography.

Thanks, also, to Laurence Ricou and Daniel Lenoski, Edward Field, and Leonard Lutwack, for their valuable work on the linkages between poetry and place; to editors of various anthologies of prairie and Alberta literature; to Sophia Isajiw and Arlene Stamp for their creative input; to Mathew Zachariah, Cecelia Frey, and the late Sharon Drummond, for their encouragement; to Walter Hildebrandt, John King, Wendy Stephens, Peter Enman, Mieka West, and Terry Ager of the University of Calgary Press; and especially to the dozens of poets included in this anthology, poets who have been writing Alberta in their own many-splendoured ways over the past several years.

Now it's time to begin our journey. Sit back, relax, and enjoy our travels through Alberta with the poets.

Robert M. Stamp
Calgary
March 2005

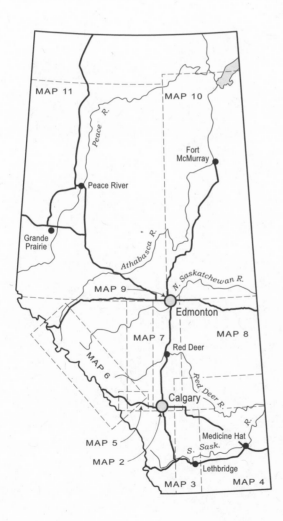

MAP 11

MAP 10

Peace R.

Fort
McMurray

Peace River

Athabasca R.

Grande
Prairie

MAP 9

N. Saskatchewan R.

Edmonton

MAP 7

MAP 8

Red Deer

MAP 6

Red Deer R.

Calgary

R.

MAP 5

Medicine Hat

S. Sask.

MAP 2

Lethbridge

MAP 3

MAP 4

Barry McKinnon

UNTITLED

living in Alberta
do you expect poems
of giant grain elevators
and miles
of golden wheat

or would you rather have
the rushing rivers
and tales of mountain ghosts

when I was six I would visit
my grandmother's farm and trek
to the coulee a mile away   always
watching for the coyotes that were
said to eat explorers   who bathed
in this prairie gorge

I could tell of the red
elevator to the north

and the worn gray fences
that would end in sunsets
further towards the city

or of the indian chief who
wanted to live in the U.S.
where the feathers of any tribe
can be a passport for beer

living in Alberta where there
is black oil
and some poets   who are afraid
of heritage   and   the quiet farms

that are part of their growth
afraid to tell because they are
not very old

living in Alberta
do you expect poems
of the golden wheat

or of how golden wheat
is now turned
to flour.

Dennis Cooley

LABIARINTH

travelling west

thru alberta this was
you could tell
everyone looked
funny everywhere you looked

hay   look Megan said
& we looked & saw
the road the road you could
see   the way was paved
way to hell & gone it was
        /paved

does Kroetsch know this
I said well actually I didnt
say this as a matter of fact I thot
about that road for a long
long time it damn near
drove me crazy

the road that long
long road was paved
every goddamn inch
                    of it

thru Alta this was
you could tell

the way was paved

I WAS BORN ALBERTA

Ribbons of liquid asphalt
and loose gravel pulse
through my veins
as I inhale this province.
Windows down, wind swept
floating permafrost roads
billow dust behind me.
Deer leap high beams
shadow in the muskeg
among stunted firs
under the kaleidoscope
of Aurora Borealis.
Golden wheat fields wave August
as oil pumps combine
harvest dreams in the palette
of a Rocky Mountain canvas.
Dinosaur and Buffalo-Smashed-In bones
fuse with mine.
Sun dried and wind scoured
they call to me
from the Hoodoos.

THE RIGHT FRAME OF MIND

> *Canada is not the land for the idle sensualist.*
> — Catharine Parr Traill

Oh god let us not be idle
look at Alberta, look at her –
her bare body rolls down sated
after the orgy of mountains
but does she stop then?
No.
her skin springs into wheat and grass
and luscious hair
wild to be combed and scratched
with the breasts and feet of sliding animals
and the giant rake of the machine
that does such things
an ecstasy of liquid willow
rubs in every fold and crevice
and in the huge bald tongue of the sky
the hawk's wing is but
a grain of salt licked off her heaving back
Oh yes.
look at the doe's wet eye,
the hairy crack of crocus,
the flagellant storm,
the veined leg of the elk,
the warm bark of the tree
that strips before the saw
and Catharine, Catharine,
tell me that
again.

IT'S THE CLIMATE

At my autopsy
they will find
my belly, intestines,
bladder & spleen
packt solid with
the flying dust of Alberta.

Charles Noble

MNEMONIC WITHOUT PORTFOLIO

The field got larger, the last field
covered with flax straw still to be burnt
for which next year we knew something different.

The neighbour came back from seeding,
stopped on the road, took his young
German shepherd out and shaved all the hair off.

While man made little black bales
the shepherd ran into our field
and rolled in the flax fire ashes.

When they left, the little bales
were stacked against a fence post
where he kept cattle.

The district all saw the little pile
and they knew exactly what it meant.

I stole the hair and pasted it on
a papier maché life-size dog,
planted it in the field for a week
then burned the effigy one night.

They all asked where in the white
canine smoke was I at.

I said I wasn't sure
since at the last election
they changed the rural/urban representation.

John O. Thompson

FUEL CRISIS

Half the time I Britishly say *petrol*,
the other half Canadianly *gas*;

say both (1973) a lot
now there's less.

Were there ever to be none at all –
my dear Alberta dry too, or withholding –
left with two names for a lack, how hard I'd find it

to choose the fittingest homonym: the state
such matter's in as, for example, the air;
or the sea bird whose epithet is *stormy*.

8

Robert Stamp

ENERGY TO BURN

Ralph Klein jets down to Washington
tells Dick Cheney
"We have energy to burn
and we are willing to share."
The premier opens the vice-president's
eyes to Alberta's tar sands
the province's willingness
to export oil and natural gas
quench the U.S. thirst
for secure energy supplies.
Ralph invites Dick to visit Alberta
see the tar sands for himself
address an international business forum
perhaps do a little fly-fishing.

(While we're at it, why not
give them our coal forests water
our brightest young graduates
first-born sons, virgin daughters
anything they want?)

Jean Chrétien trips up in Edmonton
suggests Alberta share its largesse
with the rest of the country
gives provincial politicians
apoplectic fits.
Editorials warn the prime minister
to keep his dirty hands
off Alberta's God-given resources
or we will "let the Eastern bastards
freeze in the dark."

(By the way, did Ralph
invite Jean for a friendly
eighteen holes of golf?)

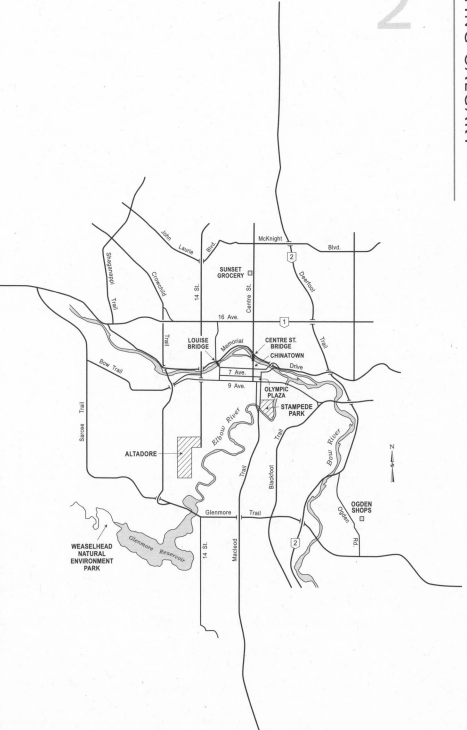

Ian Adam

IN CALGARY THESE THINGS

a collapsing house in Chinatown
      western style with verandah
and very fine around 1920.
      now the quack grass in the lawn,
a '63 Buick parked in front.
      young orientals, three of them,
stare at me.

the Queen's Hotel beer parlour,
      Indian prostitutes
shabby, squat, staring
      into half-filled glasses,
flat beer, driftwood of city.

On Crescent Road, that
      ribbon of speedway on top
of the unstable north escarpment
      of the shallow Bow river
a pheasant, scurrying across to
      shelter of the last few trees
on the bank.

last winter they found four lynx,
      three bobcats
      many coyotes
and one moose
      wandered within city limits.
on the campus you still may see
      far grouse and chicks following like a tail,
      rabbits.

my next door neighbour is a janitor
who has bought a $30,000 house.
he is not an oriental
he is not an Indian
he has stuck some plaster bunnies on his lawn

George Bowering

CALGARY

In the far west distance
the lids of mountains
        presumably the Rockies
        props for the Northern Lights

Into them
            a knife-way
        Highway One, umbilical of this town
Calgary, born by mistake
wind-built, dumped at the foot of the hills

eroded down to there
overgrown with grass
festooned with insects
roamed by prairie chickens
supporting life, people, Indians
then oilmen, football players
civil defense army, police with flashlights
professors, taxmen, lawyers, mayors
faces flashing in the Northern Lights

cutting themselves to pieces with apartments
building, sand on sand, eroding
pincht against the wind
hopeless on the wrong side of the mountains
web-footed for the sea
all these, all these, a
                        box social of a city
hoax on dumfounded prairie chickens
lost belly-button of the Kanadian west.

Murdoch Burnett

BOYS OR THE RIVER

The river that ran through my boyhood
still runs. On a hot summer night I, no longer
a child, walked the old path savouring river
muck smells and bat flight. No longer a child,
the darkened tree depths contained no
opponents ready for battle. Try as I might
I could conjure not one nazi waiting to be
dispatched with a quick blast from my mouth
sound machine gun. Now the boys in battle
carry stick lazer-guns and the sound they
make is zip. Try as I might I can't see how zip
could kill a fly. But then, I am no longer
a child. Older now than even a child's
imagining I walked along the path beside
my boyhood river and came aroun' the bend
to where the tree still stands taller than the
rest and the rope is still hanging. There in the
moonlight was a boy alone. *It might have been
streetlight, the city has changed but not boys or
the river.* He held the rope like a champion
and ran up in the air out over the river and
back to the bank in an arc of triumph so
complete he didn't need to look around to see
who watched. When I stepped from the
shadow he looked me full in the face and said,
want to try it. Of course all of us, no longer
children, know what happened. It was the
child in me the boy saw, even more clearly
than I can remember who reached up and
grabbed the rope with expert childhood
hands and fumbling adult fingers. It was the
child in me who swung like a hero out across
the boyhood river and back to the bank like
I had done it all my life. It was I, no longer

a child, who ran the wrong way and swung
like gravity to the tree.

On me there are scars now, boyhood trips and
fights and those other scars we get later.
There among them all are the scars from that
hot summer night when I made incongruous
contact with the tree still standing taller than
the rest … and the child I am no longer.

Anne Campbell

CALGARY CITY WIND

This city Calgary has a wind
        that is a peculiar kind of kid
    hanging round
              pulling at edges
      pushing fingers
                underneath loose pilings
       prying up shaky parts
                  'til finally
                     it shifts

the city is undone
                no longer fixed in soil
    but rocking
             unrooted
                 wind quickens
   puts a shoulder to the city
nudges it over
            and over it goes again
                 and again
       coming down hard
            on his own again
                  wind

is walking away
           devilish
          proud

WRITTEN ON WATER

She was a distant aunt whom we called *Gun Goo.* Honorary
name after she jumped or fell off Centre Street bridge at first
snowfall, "the dead that fly towards sunset" reminds me of
what she did which became the noun *Gun Goo* . We were
teenagers I said to my sister don't pull a *Gun Goo* the Bow
River beneath us river meaning carried away forever flippancy
helps when everything surrounds like a circular waterfall
tipping you towards its edge but the river is there and we
don't owe it anything

I brought you here where she is and I stood back then and you
said nothing among the wild rose and Indian paintbrush and
your sweater billowed like blown glass at the end of a sentence

FROM THE OGDEN SHOPS

*

> *across your ogden blue shoulders*
> *pour bleach*
> *pull money from the fire*

> *we'll hold matches to oil barrels*
> *sleep under graves bridge together*
> *clack flint together*

*

blue through blue collars
slip white over the ridge
drive gravel trucks up millican rd and reclaim lynnwood for ogden
w/ gravel from our ploughed streets
tony says chains from the king's crew
ride out of sherwood w/ bricks
downtown calgary windows w/ broke glass cuts
they run w/ busted faces down glenmore
picket placards behind
fall back
robins syphon oil w/ beaks choke sediment
into the bow

*

swords rise into the air where clouds smoke smokestack blue
mr robins cries paper into money
at the synapse snap sales counter screwdriver
tree stump page ink streets
roll through water
trestle presents factory watch if i tie your hands
to olympia dr or ogden hotel
open and blood crack paper cut
blasting cap blue your hands
to ogden rd turn gravel rd

flips gravel up to the bow
flips arrows out to downtown to get money because sidewalk cracks w/ concrete
red breast pull arrow back
sword down on glass uses bricks to break
windows w/ their own bricks

    *

trace arrows in the trees and mr robins sounds mike out
over the ridge where the bow is
howl like coyotes w/ swords haul his carcass
over the train trestles pressure twenties like insurance
forms sediment
roll rail behind ogden rd
through sherwood arrows through
key car doors that they close sherwood coins like fists
pawn fights after school
over ogden over the bow
over arrows to stop oil rail
he lets the body fall back
but in ogden the trains sun and the trains carry oil
and cars burn streets into sediment

Cecelia Frey

UNDER THE LOUISE BRIDGE

Lovers walk along the Elbow's bend
on red cinder pathways beneath leafing poplars
through wolf willow and honeysuckle
so sweet it draws bees from suburbs
Children's voices in the distance pipe thin notes
and the old couple walking before us
shade themselves with a Chinese umbrella

Indifferent to the water's flash and break
or the canoe people steering their course
paddles balanced on their knees
the lovers curl themselves into each other
their tongues searching for hollows

As they disappear into stone
you tell me of perfect arches
the beauty of mathematics
the way a curve of air supports tons of metal
ourselves in metal cages

The lovers cross the bridge
without benefit of equations, unaware
they are walking on rainbows
caught as they are
she in the curve of his shoulder
he in a loop of her spinning hair

ON A WINTER HILL OVERLOOKING CALGARY

On this silver hill the new year approaches
The night dark as carbon paper
A few brave stars weather the winter sky

Your absence
twins the cold
No one knows why I left the party

Below me gold and pewter of new city lights
sparkle with wealthy glittering eyes
University buildings twinkle with innocent brilliance

Through the window
a string of colored gowns sway like Japanese lanterns
to the bracing distant music
A woman dozes in her excessively low-stripped chair

Ice has gnawed its way into the hill's belly
Ice with the sharpness of teeth
Snow wiggles its way into my open metalic shoes

It's pointless to think of you
wrapped in the island sands of another season
It's equally pointless to freeze –
to stop my flow of blood
                for   you
                    again

I edge my sandaled steps
down the shivery hill

My flesh hesitates at the glacial knob
Lifting my velvet skirt to the doorknob
I enter the lit house
I swing the carved oak door behind me

I end the cold

Deborah Godin

TIME / LAPSE
 Calgary as Bremen

These days   after half a dozen
intervening centuries, the sun is all but set
by four o'clock
in the bitter late afternoon
a burnished disk
dispensing rosegold evenly over
the countryside and town
blue snowy roofs and sidewalks
among the evergreen spires
while /

the cold tightens its grip
mute with winter the sky listens
to the wailing voices
of ambulances echoing in between
the rows of empty office towers
the gaunt populace out dancing
in the dirty streets and littered malls
riots and fire their last acts before
crowding under the ice, quenching
their fevers in the open channel
below the stone bridge

day grows more silent   only a few hymns
left in the throats on pocked survivors
mending windows   only one chimney in ten
sends a plume up into the copper light
everywhere blunt frost obscures
details of the ravages of
time / later
on the frozen outskirts
coyotes gather to yowl
at the moon, sallow crescent
and the same hard stars blink down

WOLF WILLOW AGAINST THE BRIDGE

The City of Calgary plants it;
a hardy bush
willows against a footbridge,   overpass

butter blooms in silver-green
hard candy pebbles of sweet feral
                    Wolf Willow

Crushed against this bridge,
willow of your hard brown body
                immovable; the taste
of you in May

Silver-green and offering me
            tart willow buds

that drip from my hair
driving past the bridge –
                a scent
                of you

Robert Hilles

WHEN LIGHT TRANSFORMS FLESH
(*Bow River, Calgary*)

A river passes here every day. Its water seeks the soft shores
at night, drinking the earth like a child drinks Kool-aid. The
river has dreams too as it passes downtown making the
high-rises into liquid. Lovers have walked its shore until their
bodies have seized water and air. In the streets, others have
forgotten the river. Drinking different water treated against a
civilization of microbes. Still the river passes neglected and
feared. The rocks below twisting in a mad dance. The air so
cold beneath the surface it freezes in small pockets. Death is
the responsibility of water. The river serving as a chilled
entrance. You may wonder why there are few trees along its
massive shore. You may find yourself wanting to walk across
it at its shallowest point. A river passes here each day and
nothing is impossible. Let the lovers show you what the
water means.

CALGARY MIRAGE

when we first came here we
bought a bed
a kitchen
and cooked visions

in the mornings
the mountains
crumbly pie crust
on the horizon
the glazed hills swirled and peaked
like soft meringue
the city boiled with people
bubbled with cars and buildings
like a glistening filling
erupting from
the sweet scoops of hill

mouthwatering potential

now my hands pick at the dry sheets
the kitchen windows are dark with grease

this is a high altitude desert
the wind panting at our roof
and drought crawling
into our lawn

Bruce Hunter

WISHBONE

in these most drunken moments
i am convinced
by my halfbreed friends
that in the other life
even before their brothers and mine
roamed the gullies
in search of the last wild pony
in those years before
i was bear
with great demon eyes
toothed of lightning

this life instead
sentenced to bar room glory
as a man
a small man at that
to remember that bulldozers
have piled bones
under trails taken from your names
Deerfoot, Shaganappi, Crowchild
paved four lanes wide
carrying others whose tongues
are awkward to your names

small man
wishing to be bear again
rake men to blood
test skulls between his teeth

Pauline Johnson

CALGARY OF THE PLAINS

Not of the seething cities with their swarming human hives,
Their fetid airs their reeking streets, their dwarfed and poisoned lives,
Not of the buried yesterdays, but of the days to be,
the glory and the gateway of the yellow West is she.

The Northern Lights dance down her plains with soft and silvery feet.
The sunrise gilds her prairies when the dawn and daylight meet;
Along her level lands the fitful southern breezes sweep,
And beyond her western windows the sublime old mountains sleep.

The Redman haunts her portals, and the Paleface treads her streets,
The Indian's stealthy footstep with the course of commerce meets,
And hunters whisper vaguely of the half forgotten tales
Of phantom herds of bison lurking on her midnight trails.

Not hers the lore of olden lands, their laurels and their bays;
But what are these, compared to one of all her perfect days?
For naught can buy the jewel that upon her forehead lies –
The cloudless sapphire Heaven of her territorial skies.

Robert Kroetsch

HORSETAIL SONNET

Under the sun-bleached towers the ghost city
that Brisebois named for himself, the city
of horses and badger holes, the cryptic city

built on a hidden field of buffalo beans
and lupines,
              tells of cowboy girls in jeans
and lariats to rope the towers' bones.

Speculators, not to mention theater managers,
bank executives and forest rangers,
along with aging poets and other scroungers

never look down. For fear of falling, that is.
For fear of the branding iron's hiss.
For fear, possibly, of a well-aimed kiss.

The carnage of the bull's behind is referendum
on ascent. Fix not the tail and scrotum
to a star. Just tell the dog, go get 'em.

Erin Michie

THE WILLOWS AT WEASELHEAD

Last time I was here, a coyote gave me a backward glance.

Power lines, fences, a paved path. Signs: speed limits, horses here,
bikes there, no dogs beyond this point, future site of Sarcee trail
extension, bear country, high pressure gas pipeline.

Raven song throats through a flat February's
rumpled hillsides, last year's wrinkled rosehips.
Spruce silhouette and poplars bending.

The willows are bold here, all red and cognizant.
The willows knew
about today's snow.

Almost a foot! I join my retired neighbours across the street in a
spontaneous shovelling bee. I do John's sidewalk beside mine,
cross to help Jim and Rena, then all of us do Margaret's while
she's clearing her driveway. Her husband inside with Parkinson's,
her grateful, English voice.

Jim and Rena invite me in, John joins us, hair wavy silver,
quickly combed before coffee. The three of them with mugs of
instant, my cup and saucer peppermint tea.

They tease, talk tomatoes, John's brother's terminal cancer and
Rena's ornery aunt. John shrugs death into life.

Snow slowing down, barely perceptible flakes.

Deborah Miller

PICTURES FROM THE STAMPEDE

On the way a small band of Indians
on horseback on Macleod Trail
in restored native dress. One man
with a bandage over his nose,
as if he'd just had rhinoplasty,
and one moviestar chief dropped
his arm from the reins to gather me
up on his steed. When they passed
I couldn't stop crying then laughing,
said to Jay, *God I'm a downer eh?*

Zambora the gorilla girl
from "Nairobi in deepest darkest
Africa forced to undergo
horrible medical experiments"
made her look like a teenager
wearing black leotards. Later
she transformed into a gorilla
two feet taller than she was
three seconds before.

The 4H Club Princess wore
a blue satin gown, crown and running
shoes. Quickly she tried to tie
the miniature horse to its tiny coach
but it reared up twice. She slapped it
on the side of the face hard.
Both contestants were pissed off.

Two kids on the bumper cars
doing the forbidden head on collision.
The under-barker telling us he loved
his job because he could hit anybody he liked.
We promised we wouldn't give him any trouble.

31

Hey I know man, I didn't mean you guys.
The underblond barker smiled then turned
away to knock down some rowdy four year old.

In the barn a woman fried up fresh pork patties
one stall over from four suckling piglets
and their momma. I will never eat meat again.
Carnival filth and ear-bleeding music
thick on our bodies. Fifteen minutes
later Jay and I split
a big beef rib dinner for ten dollars.
It was good.

James M. Moir

THIS CITY BY THE BOW

Who could have predicted this melange –
bushy-haired writers
performing poets
ego graduates
solemn professors
new plutocrats
young clerks
night workers
and tall cowboys
in Stetsons and spurs?
To attract them we built
this city by the Bow
this conglomeration
of streets and houses
skyscrapers
traffic jams   garbage trucks
muggers   hookers
and yellow fire hydrants
eyed by wandering dogs.
Collectively they reach
so   greedily toward the mountains
that the green world around
is shouldered aside.
Do not forget that
beyond these streets
there is a great bowl of sunlight
in the blue afternoon of sky
an arrangement
of green grass   purple mountains
bay horses and
                    red barns

Colin Morton

CALGARY '80

the pink ladies and the couriair
cars prowl seventh avenue
between open pits and cable spools

THE CASE OF THE DISAPPEARING SIDEWALK!

on this corner
frog-throated boys used to sing
                    CALGARY HERALD PAPER
                    LATE CITY EDITION
                    HERALD PAPER
and give change from their aprons with sharp-eyed
fingers,
            where today
an acre of glass encases
a twelve-month garden
frequented by popcorn bags and exotic birds
I can't hear from the street,

                    and drill bits
                    all sizes
                sexy and primitive:

                office ornaments
                paper weights
                garden fountains

                    drill bits
                drill bits have balls

        THIS IS A HARDHAT AREA
        NO HELP NEEDED

34

across from this sign I stand a half hour
to see how many Ontario dropouts
come looking for employment:
                                no one
loiters around the jobsite,
everyone hurries by
carrying briefcases, money sacks, takeout food,

no one walks by as if they had the day off,
no one is retired or too young to work,

even I can't stand here idle, I take notes,
I tell myself, must be a working writer,
must take notes wherever I go,
then I'll find out
where the sidewalks went.

Erin Mouré

SOUTH-WEST, OR ALTADORE

Our imperfect, fleeting minds.
The woman about to begin
her walk thru the desert, carrying
a small suitcase with the words
"Eleftherias Street," folded, inside.
Already, I am full of such bitterness for my life.
I am young, & bitterness is the quarry
of the young.
The street is long, the light thin.
The brown of the grass, after so many,
the white of the fence, sings.
So cold.
As if, the prefiguration of snow.
The drink of light wine hurting
the chest. *Típota.*

2

Those of us who remain calm
that is to say, angry
Those of us who are enraged,
& thus can eat, holding the fork up
with the food, pushing our heads
forward, bird-like, eating
Those of us who have had enough
Those of us *qui sont tannées*
Eating
Forging the food into the liquid of the body
The liquid so dense & pure
there could be no end to tears
should we begin them

But we won't
Those of us who are displaced
from the measure

Those of us who are here tonight
I bow to us with all my cutlery
Beware us
Those of us who remain clam

   3
Going into what desert, south-
west
Calgary Alberta, or
Altadore, 16th St & 36th Ave,
the dead end & box apartments,
the huge blinking light of Safeway,
the concrete wall
Going in to the desert
carrying the suitcase, a weight
of dream
Its silk empty
The rabbit gun against the house wall, loaded
Cold air & a view of the mountains
Bright sun on the stucco wall

   4
The woman unfolding the page on which is written:
οδ·ελευθερια
That's it, the line.
How long can we live before we die.
As if, all women, carry
the light of the south-west: doorsnowdoorsnowdoor
The noise of this.
She gets up, out of her chair

once in every poem, adjusting the slatted blind
to let the snow in.

5
The cat howls.
The dessert on the table (compote de poires) howls.
The compote de poires howls.
The applesauce howls.
The table is starting
howling
I've had it
Shut up, everything

6
What you would take into the desert or,
if not available, the mountains: a compass,
waterproof matches, a groundsheet.
Hard boots, broken in. In which
the past steps of the being

howl

7
the winds here   *northern*
The body with its fabled warmth lifts up
we say
the heart. The worn tree-line above which
the flat light of the avenue.
The mountains/desert finally
the same place
The shutting of the house door
to go off & wage the self
against the hinge of a single word
Eleftherias

& stand up, our desert equipment
softened
Our chests speaking to us in a murmur
Our neighbours who are carpenters
We hear them at night in their finest dresses
dancing   *snowdoor*
after so much silence
Their gestures

at the heart of Altadore,   inside us ....

BECAUSE CALGARY

Downtown. 7th Ave. and 1st St. s.e., behind the LRT tracks. Look
for Thi's Canada. The Regis Hotel. Strippers. Out of a cab a
woman in short tight skirt. Zipper up the back, hem to waistband.
Man too thin leans against brick, horks. Could be my uncle.
Windows upstairs, all highrised Calgary in panes. Look for Thi's
Canada. My grandfather in one of those rooms died drunk …

    *

Again on the sidewalk in front of the Regis. Thinking of Thi. And
a man crutches toward me, hey sister could you give me some
money I got in an accident and I got to go home to my reserve but
I got no money for the bus, booze on his breath swaying and I am
caught (four alcoholic uncles on my mother's side), give him the
money (the youngest gave me two hundred dollars once) or say no
(when he drank he shit himself) or call the Friendship Centre to
ask for advice when the man swipes at my face. Cheap bitch …

    *

Along the Bow River. Walking. Cottonwood, willow, goose shit.
Canada? Christ, how about Calgary, one street even, one
building. The bus barn one block south of the Bow, across from
Eau Claire Lumber office now a restaurant, breakfast all day.
Diesel, oil on cement. Lay in a trench, fiddled in the guts of a bus.
Mother's father. Sober, good friend, good buddy. Piss drunk.
Passed out. Canned. One week later and only a red brick chimney
left. Hole in the ground, and rocks. For a big friggin hotel and
market. Covered so the vegetables don't get rained on ….

Robert Stamp

A CITY BUILT FOR SPEED

every day from every corner
of this sprawling city
they attack downtown
on c-trains from Whitehorn
buses from Altadore and Coach Hill
cyclists on the Bow River Pathway

and by car
thousands thousands of cars
cars from residential streets
shift onto arterial roads
storm Deerfoot Trail
swoop across Langevin Bridge

wave after wave
oil-patch executives
high-tech workers
shoppers, students
a ceaseless stream
of solitary drivers
Calgary

1912

There is power
in Calgary
Lights in windows
that have nothing to do
with reflections
from moon or stars or sun

Power
in Calgary
and none of it
carried in the bag
of the Medicine Man
or in the wisdom
of the chief

Hydro-electricity
I am told
is as easy to understand
as a current of flowing water
There is power here
In this city it will
never be night again.

QUADRANT FOUR – OUTSKIRTS OF OUTSKIRTS
(*from* Calgary, this growing graveyard)

Calgary as quadrant, the sweep of a long-armed compass quartering
the city NW NE SE SW, segmented.

Each quadrant leaks outward up the hills, along the coulees in a
sprawl of roofs.

But the north side accidental, begun by squatters/the first wave
immigrants, Germans and Italians, brothels to the east.

The REAL city south, inched its way southward, money and business
moving down from the low and gravelled Bow. No
designations needed there, neither SW or SE until years later, it
was the north that needed division and indication, North
beyond, over the river, squatters and whores.

The divisions/labyrinthine begun.

And when they talked "annex" NW kept at arm's length, safely out
there.

Offered the streets names:

Aaron/Jacob/Joshua/
(him again)
Matthew/Mark/Luke/John/
Esther/Sarah/Moses/Mark/
Jeremiah

proper names of biblical intention, but subsumed
(1912)
by numbers, the sweet anonymity of 6th. Only Kensington left
unnumbered and itself.

An acroustic of place, 4th St. S.E. far away from 4th St. N.W.
divided into quarters and beyond the quarters suburbs themselves
divided and names picked up from the subdivisions.

There has to be a minotaur somewhere.

How to find yourself: see map.

A majority of roads are named by number.

Within the quadrantic network 14th Ave. N.W. will run east-west in
the north west quadrant.

Where is home?

But from the outside, as early wo
(man)
a nomad wandering the prairie?

From Nightingale east, moving west toward only a cleft in the hills,
no evidence of city. And the pretence of buildings a slight
inflection that swells as the body moves. The mountains
overweigh all and only when you dip south into the valley of
the Bow the gaunt buildings appear, innocuous from this angle
buried in themselves. And black. Unless you are at exactly the
right hillcrest at dawn enigmatic and unreflective, none of the
golden flash that you expect.

From High River south, the old 2A leading itself north into
appropriation, and the curve of the double road that splits the
collective huddled suburbicarian purlieus, outskirts of outskirts
outskirted by those same foothills
(are we in Lethbridge yet?)
The overflung devouring edges stitching themselves into the
ground.

The ground, that yellow and black prairie ground between the
fingers crumbling and soft. The foothills/foreland thrust sheets.

And in your swing up through Millarville, Priddis, Bragg Creek and
Morley the fortress begins to tower and sway, sown dragon's
teeth that have grown themselves into monoliths without the
sacred sites at their bases, without pictographs and secret
springs, and *Uluru*
(that red nose in the Australian desert)
complete in their unscalability.

Except for the window washers
(of course)
Except for the falling accountants, except for the clefts and
ledges of hurt that have all been smoothed down, polished over
into a flat blank surface, refracting only itself. You too can
jump.

And from the
(north)
bush and parkland, Bashaw, Tees, Lacombe,
(who taught you to forget Siksika)
Olds and Didsbury and Carstairs a descent.

That snaky arrival between the sexual clefts of the hills again
surprised at the arrogance of those other coulees brooding in on
themselves in a pretence at centre, an underground that repels.

Calgary is a place to run away from, although you claim to have run
to it. And everyone claims to be from somewhere else, not
here, no babies born in this city except reluctantly, extracted
from their mothers' bodies in a storm of protest. Most children
born in moving vehicles:

the c-train
buses
pickup trucks
(inevitable gun racks)
moving vans

An acroustic of place: If there were time to count muffler shops and
Sleepeazy motels, faster and faster food and the secret motives
of car dealerships
(pricing themselves on windshields)
you would never be found. Again.

But there are labyrinths in the shopping malls, bubbles of light and
air that claim closure, insist on wholeness and order, and you
wandering, lost, cannot find the door you came in or any door
at all and behind the shop window mannequins there is nothing:
darkness, a bed, a small room full of stifled
whispers that pretend to be obscene.

Strip malls too: a dry cleaners, a Chinese restaurant, an uncrashed
    bank pasting themselves onto the crossword puzzle of street.

    And behind their plate glass only darkness, a winnowed square
    of space that offers sleep and dreams, a queer fishbowl silence
    from the shrieking air outside.

You begin to look for lovers in these labyrinths of solar light.
    In the secret floors of hotel rooms, hotels interlocked by Plus
    15s, ghostly vaginas:

    In one green room you bathe together, splash each other.
    In another you lie side by side, breathing gently.
    You are seldom locked together, sex is too playful for Jericho
    and two pieces of the puzzle might connect.

    What would happen then – all the interlocking bridges
    (Louise and Langevin)
    (Louise should really be buried)
    unnecessary
    – all the trails
    (Crowchild, Marquis de Lorne, Shaganappi, Deerfoot)
    overruled, all 3000 kilometres of paved road bypassed in a
    flyover of lust, for once lust.

You need practice in the geography of lust.

You need to find lovers in used bookstores
    take someone else's clothes from the cleaners
    invade the bushes of Spruce Cliff.

There are incipient connections between lonely watchers at the
    Plaza and in the playgrounds bodies lying on their backs in the
    grass. Snow bodies.

Freeways stop abruptly, refuse to handle themselves into the hills
    farther than they are, abandonment in a fringe of crumbling
    asphalt.

Plus 15s drop into space and connect nothing.

Paths lead a darkness of wooded coulee impossible to return from.

46

Mud rooms front the marble foyers of post-modern buildings,
    log houses hewn into modern pretence a visceral cry against
    glass.

Who can find you here, a clumsy bawling beast in the centre of a
    web of thread, a cat's cradle of encapturement?

Located by confluence, the Bow and Elbow jointing themselves in
    an impassable lock. Without their deliberated quadrant you
    scramble in hollow streets and scanty hills, looking to the
    escarpment above, the sharp edge of Shaganappi coulee cutting
    off the mountains.

In the squats and dry electricity of basement flats where printmakers
    select inks and artists draw faces
    (faces of women looking sidelong at one another)
    in the quarrels of the colleges and schools students foundering
    into a sadly chosen ritual, there is still the labyrinth of stone.

The fossils of lost centuries embedded in walls, an
    architect's drawing of place. Brachiopods shine through their
    sealed surface, erypsids genuflect.

You too sheathed in prehistoric stone, the gravestones of Jericho
    before the walls tumble down.

Shout Calgary.

Wilfred Watson

IN THE CEMETERY OF THE SUN

For the first Monday of my week
Of darkness came May's last month. October
Wrath of Mayspring breathed on a smoulder
Of chrysanthemum, till it was dark
Shrivel, till it was the first sun
Of frost, till the cold of my fever
Breathed in the octave and after
Of the saintspring and feast of May,
Dry and dry its weather of leaves,
Dry and cold and dry its flower,
In the toward and paltry of death's unnecessary

There stood the skullbrow of my death's
Hill (and I saw seven partridge
In a brown apparition walk across
My grave of grass, my prairie of grave,
Birds of the earth made gross for winter,
Their fat breast bosomed in the sun's
Light, though the darkness of my hill was
Fat behind them, as they walked across
My morning and went) till my last day

Sang into my eyes. In the cemetery of the sun below
All the houses of the living were tombs;
And I saw Calgary a hill of tombstones
Rising under a coast of mountains
Washed in the cold of my sun of cloud.
When I walked to the wither of my day
In this city where every backyard had
Its cross and clothesline white and sere
With sereclothes shining in the sun
Of my first despair of resurrection

Came my first Monday of darkness. It
Was the week's hanging and drying noon.
All the drought of my bones was for water.
And the ghosts of my people flapped about
Me in this washday blow and weather.
But though I bent in the drown of sun
To the mutter of sleeve and sheet
I could not find the heart or answer
To answer that morning the winter
Upstart and May of this October
Wording me even to the spring of doom.

CALGARY 2 A.M.

In spite of the fact that it is twenty below
and the winter has lasted six months

in spite of being starved   starved almost to death
for greenness and warmth   flowers and birds

in spite of the deadness of endless classrooms
shopping centres   television programmes

in spite of the pains in the gut   the migraines
the wakings   the palpitations

in spite of the sickening knowledge of laziness
of failure to meet obligations

in spite of all these things   and more
I have to report that the moon tonight

is filling the house with a wild blueness
my children grow   excel   are healthy

my wife is gentle   there are friends
and once in a while a poem will come

In spite of the fact that it is twenty below
tonight I smile   Summer bursts inside me

Rita Wong

SUNSET GROCERY

at eight years old the cash register's metallic rhythm comes quick to
my fingers: 59¢ from $1.00 gets you back one penny, one nickel, one
dime, one quarter. could do this backwards in my sleep, & probably
have, but i prefer stocking shelves. prefer to avoid customers making
snotty fake chinese accents, avoid men flipping through porn.
open nine to nine seven days a week, the store is where i develop
the expected math skills: $60 net one day divided by
twelve hours is $5 an hour, divided by two people is
$2.50 an hour, or divided by five
people $1.00 an hour.

occupied with small details, sunset grocery can be duller
than counting the 20,000 times i breathe each day. i sell
cigarettes i am not allowed to smoke: player's light,
export a, du maurier. nicotine variations, drum &
old port. popsicles, twinkies, two percent milk. 7-up,
coffee crisp, bottles of coke. faced with these cancer-&
cavity-inducing goods, i retreat into books. by grade four
i learn the word "inscrutable" & practice being so
behind the cash register. however, i soon realize that i
am read as inscrutable by many customers with absolutely
no effort on my part, so i don't bother trying any more ....

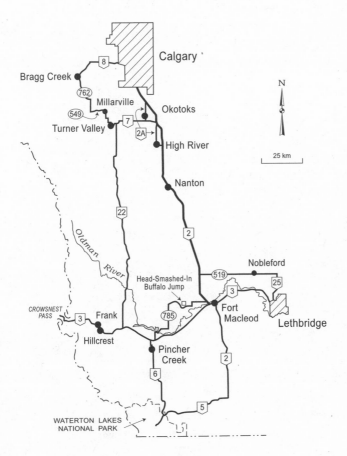

Calgary

Bragg Creek

8

762

Millarville

549

Turner Valley

7

Okotoks

2A

High River

Nanton

22

2

Oldman River

Nobleford

519

25

Head-Smashed-In
Buffalo Jump

3

CROWSNEST
PASS

3

Frank

785

Fort
Macleod

Hillcrest

Lethbridge

Pincher
Creek

2

6

5

WATERTON LAKES
NATIONAL PARK

N

25 km

D.C. Reid

DRYING OUT AGAIN

Like a young boy unfairly treated,
Daddy takes off forever in his Lincoln.
With a trusty fifth of vodka
he rides beside the sunset:
Okotoks, Nanton, Claresholm.
Seventy miles an hour across the flatness that is Alberta,
prairie wool bruised by sun.
Windows slide closed on his own little fish bowl.
His world is airconditioned, quadraphonic:
Barbara Streisand's richness a quixotic liquid in his head.
Tears course freely down unruly creases
that years of booze have cut in his suntanned face.
A millionaire business genius from his bootstraps up.
Savvy for bucks and a hole in his confidence
he can drive his whole life through
and not fill with success or the music of booze.
He's been recovering for decades
patched his life on a jet from here to anywhere.
Never slowed down long enough to break
from little boy needs
beaten inside by the charming bastard he called father.
He'll show 'em. Give up booze
face his crumbled world; children, business, wife lost
trying to prove he's good as the next guy.
He'll pull a rabbit out of a hat
drive south to the sanatorium
through winding hills, rings of smoke.

THE BIG ROCKS

as you look from the distance
approaching from Okotoks
they sit out on the field,
like two marbles.
nearing,
you sense the mighty hand that has rolled them
then pushed them halfway into the earth.

closer, you have to open the fence gate,
walk across the field, stubble now,
littered with cowshit from the winter,
more concentrated near the rocks,
especially on the south side
where the cattle have sheltered through
the bitter northern winds and storms.

the same blasts once built
the glaciers that found these rocks in the
                                        mountains,
inched them slowly down the ranges
of geologic time
from the place we call Jasper
but to which our labels
are about as permanent
as the spray painting of
Harry and Wilma, May 16, 1978.

we see that they are crumbling slowly,
that steady erosion has cracked one.
go between the gap, you sense
a narrow mountain pass, the prairie
disappears in cool verticals.

the mountaineering club is practicing on them,
intent on conquests.

George Bowering

HIGH RIVER, ALBERTA

The drugstore ceiling is moulded plaster
made in a week many years ago
when the CPR tracks
were attracting people north

Mounties & priests, curious braves
guarding the peaceful grass
turned under the chunky black dirt
falling in the shade of grain elevators

Cows discovered the big country
bringing men with them, horses
to mount the Indians
& carry them into the Rockies

Now they never come back
but move south along the pike
eight miles from town
as the country moves

It's a pleasant town yet
curiously old in new Alberta
one side of a main street
false fronted against a railroad

no passengers watch from

Cecelia Frey

WOMAN IN A POTATO FIELD NORTH OF NANTON

Over a rise
driving along one of those prairie roads
that go on and on forever
later October and things dormant
suddenly
a black figure

it is nearly dark
snow swirls
            veil or shroud
revolves
                a face
            one blank eye

she wears a cost
        voluminous as wings
and rubber boots
            perched as hooked claw

on her head a babushka
        flares and ruffles
beneath her chin she ties
        flap like wattles

I recall one of Odin's two black ravens
memory on its daily task
to circle the world
and bring back the news

now she folds her feathers down
around these shrivelled hills
her darting eye routs out the potatoes
   some already lush with maggots
her talons plough this hard ground

she straightens
     bends
straightens again
     again bends
  as wings of legends
      shape the night
she creates the wind
    raw and turning blustery from the north

Sheri-D Wilson

▶

HE WENT BY JOE

and you are here with me
buffalo ghost in foothills
an oldness on my lips
a bend in a tree
by the river the cool water
on a moon-full night

and you are here with me
running with the children in moccasins
watching PowWow dancers
your name would have been Joe
the light shadows, you know
you never got to kick me
never heard your heart

and you are here with me
as grave robbers dig with their hands
and shade remembers your name
the river carries us along
she carries us along
the slippery stones of her skin

and you are here with me
Head-Smashed-In Buffalo Jump
you are here with me
watching centuries ease into twilight
you are here
under branches between pines

how old would you be?
at this gathering under blue water skies
how old would you be?
in this joy I see clear through
to the bottom
how old would you be?
in this pond full of sky

there is no prayer
just a little song that keeps singing
you are here

Charles Noble

PROPS

I'm swathing west of the house
taking my pleasure in larger cycles
patiently doing the rounds on this 135 acre field
of spring wheat in the early fall
but I have to question now
all this cutting and leaving in limbo.

And the older question of the most important
working condition – is it meaningful
and therefore in the Marx*sixth* sense
does it *make sense* in the world
so that these cycle analytics I'm seeing
curl down to senses sensing the rattle
that ends in the tiniest, most quiet
bite of the future underlying the vision
the world assumes in the spectacle of all there is?

Privilege is the fulfillment of this condition
and if we want to argue, here is where we start – at this *working*
condition cum truest privilege,
with one twist – where is the underwriter
of this lightning halflife spiral
and later thundering rainbow rings?

These one hundred and thirty-five acres
are a day at most, are a gauge
in one four wheel drive diesel, are six
miles an hour differentiating/integrating sickle eyes.

These hundred and thirty-five acres
are counted kernels in a stock exchange
cock-fight-pit of tiddly winking stars
configandthunderationfused ....

Stacie Wolfer

LETHBRIDGE

Will I miss the coulees
when I leave

these hills
sun stretching and yawning
across them at dawn

Highlighting
each mound and hill
every blade of grass

moving my hands
across their shape
caressing
buttocks or breasts
wind
slithers through my hair

gophers
tickling the belly of the coulees
as they run
peek
and chirp
through grass and shrubs

geese
perpetual mates
their trumpeting
awakens me
and the sun
we both rise
to smell earthy breath
of land
rising and falling
for a thousand years

Will I miss you
when I leave

Will I forget
unborn children
dancing in shadows
of your eyes

I give your memory away
the coulees I will keep

Karen Solie

JAVA SHOP, FORT MACLEOD

From the highway, a signal fire on the verge of prairie
so long in half light now that it is autumn.
This is a place you know to stop moving,
the tired joy of a door where you left it
and the Oldman Valley burning orange,
all your finest summers in its leaves.
It's a hinge of worlds, for you have loved poorly now
on both sides of the foothills.

Inside, frying is a kind of weather, a Florida
for flies, the doughnuts afflicted,
the coffee malicious.
Tiny friendless salads make you weep.
You've missed him by 15 years; he rested here
travelling west one summer of his life
before you. Build him out of cigarettes,
lousy tap water, what you know of his arms
and the things he looked out on. Much of it is gone.
Lean on the past and it gives. A small grace.

When it's dark, head east
past the horse killing plant. No deer for miles.
You left a line or two in the water
farther up the valley,
though someone else lives in your house.
Cross a friend's threshold and aging passes
like an unkind word between you.
Nostalgia is a prettier season. Leaves
fall on the river and a few are the colour of wine.

Sid Marty

DEATHSONG FOR THE OLDMAN RIVER

Down by the river, she bent to swim
where limestone dipped to lead us in
Raspberries roll down on the banks
and everything that lives, gives thanks

Our ponies wondered, as we stripped
I held some berries to her lips
Painted a turtle on her thigh
Our laughter echoed from cliff to cliff

Last summer, by the Oldman River
Gifts that were stolen
from the hands of the Giver

Because my mouth was drought so dry
that no water satisfied
she pressed the berries on my tongue
and on her lips I tasted them

Then we rolled in the water down to the sand
to the painted gravel where the rainbows spawn
the red paint melted in the flood
She held me there in another mood

Last summer, by the Oldman River
Gifts that were stolen
from the hands of the Giver

Raspberry mouth in the river's lift
Rosehips pointing her lovely breasts
The blue river in her eyes
as the water laughed and cried

And our ponies stood listening
As a voice, in the Earth, began to sing

Michael Cullen

WIND DOWN WATERTON LAKES

the vortex of the wind
down the first valley
an introvert
quiet, unpretentious
calmly down valleys that end
down canyons that deadend
over hills that turn to sleek granite mountains
picking up velocity
and power
rebounding from swirling arenas
back to the first valley.
in anger building and building
down the lake like an early explorer
building into the twentieth century
quietly, gaining an authority
the calm lake building whitecaps
dipping and smashing
and crashing
where once was a slick silence
and over the prairie
the mountains a funnel for the first settlers
for the first wind
onto the empty prairie steppes
raging and swirling
heavy topsoil into hidden ravines
across the desert
with an angry swirling insistence .....
dollyvardin at the bottom of the deep lake
jumping in delight
at the awesome display
at skyhooks where bait
is man bending
where master is wind
tricked into rage

Ian Adam

JOB DESCRIPTION

in Pincher Creek work building highways
play ball in the park Sundays
read Tennyson's *Idylls*,
which is supposed to be good poetry,
discover it is,
there is a Marxist trucker I argue with
and others with jokes of indescribable filth
in which we wallow,

have a one-legged roommate, enjoys being the hero
of his own particular story,
hops around in his shorts
women go for him he says
there is something about him he says.
he reads *True West* magazine.

to the southwest the ranches
homes sprawled haciendahed
verandas and creeper covered,
the wives are ladies and read Charles Dickens,
the men talk cattle and politics,
they hate all government,

northwest the coal mines,
black-smeared impoverished towns,
the earth probed through narrow shafts
where men hack out a sustenance:
they drink in beer parlours, wild unionists all,
fold dollar bills to show the dark shadow:
"Look! the Queen's asshole!"
on the road the fields yellow with mustard
wild rose scents in the valleys
make you drunk as all the bees,
ride in the blade winnowing gravel
count the trucks as they dump their loads
government checker in the warmth of the morning.

eat suppers in the restaurant
which is the setting for Hemingway's *The Killers*,
it is run by the Changs,
walk their daughter home
over the bridge and along the creek,
talk, I call her "Dragon Lady."

Jan Boydol

COLOR HILLCREST DEAD

monochroma mood
explodes
cerebral dreams
focus on
Hillcrest mine
imagine
fathers
parallel
grandfathers
gestural strokes
stain the surface of
grey rock
complementary colliery systems
collide with red
soil yellow calypsos violet orchids
scrumbling creamy layers of
bones
surface primed for
black
solitary light
struggles day to day
to begin with no one in the town slept

Aislinn Hunter

FRANK SLIDE, ALBERTA

You will hover above that town
all your afterlife, almost touching,
and remember, it was there we planted
clusters of snap-dragons and tulips,
and above us, burrowed under
the eavestrough spout,
a hornets' nest buzzed furiously
through summer.
And you, earth-stained
in the garden, hoe in hand, laughing
said you didn't have the heart
to knock it down.
Savoured the clipped sound
of their stingers against the kitchen glass,
like the small stones I'd thrown
up to your bedroom window
from your parents' front yard.

That summer the morning glory
overtook everything
and you spent hours untangling
the open blossoms, one from the other.

We were nothing next to that power,
swell of earth upturned –
and I choose to imagine you were
wrapped warm in the light
blue sheets you'd taken off the line,
smell of field grass still in them.
It was as if the ground gave
a great yawn at the end of an evening
before slumber.
And then a blanket, and under
the stony plain not a murmur or sigh.
Even the flowers bowing down
to a new loneliness.

THIS WAY CROWSNEST IS →

seven sisters watch
fascination with trains
breath in the cold morning air
envelopes
narrative frames without glue
pulp in the orange juice
empty towns
interrogation of strangers
laptops
coffee weak enough to see thru
charms to stop the rain
wild purple orchids un-named
coal pull from ground left under foot
asking the final score
late night drink/talk
mountains
words taken to the literal meaning
word ties elk and bears
mass graves
three men in a pickup without destination just determination
green hotel
the red spades
winnipegedmontonvancouverchasemontreallondonlethbridgecalgary
blairmorehillcrestlillecolemanbellevuefrank
crowsnest is
        this way →
crowsnest is this
           way →
               this way to the border this way to what
               this way simply dont know where goes
               this way this way this way this to anger
               simply dont know this anger in the
               centre of this poem in the centre dont
               want to be in the centre leave me on the

outskirts leave me on the edge leave
me leave me leave me marginal

cant be on the margins
cant be the red spade
dig with the red spade
see whats found
lost space lost letter somewhere in the
middle of this lost space is the location
of location of place this is not an empty
space this is crowsnest this is lille dont
care if there are no people now the
location exists in the memory in the
snap shots in the only names left on the
broken bricks no doubt this was once
someones

again the difficulty of space the difficulty of location the difficulty of place outside
the room seven sisters watch over the lost names of the lost faces

no picture of sid
the one
who stopped
the train
frank slide 1903
gone
but not

for
get the space
for
get the word

Ken Rivard

TURNER VALLEY

in the grasp of his hand
leaves cup color
huddling their veins
from Rocky Mountain breathing.

Turner is really a gas station philosopher
spending days in a rocking chair
studying out-of-town licence plates.

often he points to earth torches
flaming residue of oil men
from thirty years ago.
he laughs at those
who dug their wisdom into soil
soon discovering that his skin
was beginning to wear more often
an overcoat of November night.
he tells me his wide place in the road
needed that kind of protection.

but wait
look
he is walking away from me
to lead his residents to forget
what I pretend to know;
people here need more time
to finger count harvest flecks
in the trees that were once his.

Allan Serafino

HAY ROLLS NEAR MILLARVILLE

Overnight, they arrive on fields unseen,
save by some incurious cow,
hover gently over our houses
where we toss fitfully in sleep.
They feed quietly on our exhaled dreams.

And now the daytime fields are ripe
with them, large green rolls of hay,
mute pods, rich and real
in the bright sunlight, pregnant
with the weight of earthly paradises.

But tonight, as we sleep again,
they lift off without us
and in their particular rolling fashion
move as quietly as they'd come,
their harvest done,
back to the fields of Elysium.

MOUNTAIN INTERVAL II:
  Pow Wow at Bragg Creek

I compose
grasses
turn words
on a loom
thread the yellow
of sun through needles
of sharp
mountain moonlight

  2
I sing the flow
of golden streams
over ochre pathways
the fingers
of gravity in
the infinite pools,
the yielding of
marsh grass
to the forces
of water

  3
I sing the snowy
smile of mountains
over hazy plains
over sweetgrass meadows
that sleep like
children under
skies and rains

4

My sleep is
dreamless
bound with belts
and crossed with
beads,
swift coyote tails
fly past with
the wind

5

I am dizzied
by bird faces
owl masks and eagles
in endless procession
I am deafened by
drumbeats blinded
by dust
and the swoop of
the dancers

6

They circle
and move
in their shining
numbers in their
myriad thousands,
thundering ravens

7
Dust rises
and falls
its clouds cloak
the dancers
until tireless
they ride
away into distance

8
They disappear
and are lost
on the shimmering
roads

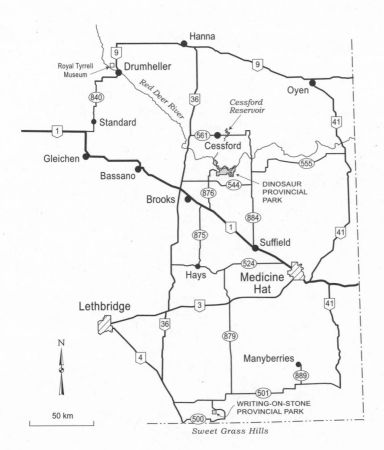

Hanna

Royal Tyrrell
Museum

9

Drumheller

840

Red Deer River

36

Standard

Cessford
Reservoir

1

561

Cessford

9

Oyen

41

Gleichen

Bassano

Brooks

876

544

DINOSAUR
PROVINCIAL
PARK

555

875

1

884

Suffield

41

Hays

524

Medicine
Hat

Lethbridge

3

36

879

41

N

4

Manyberries

889

501

WRITING-ON-STONE
PROVINCIAL PARK

500

50 km

Sweet Grass Hills

Joan Crate

GLEICHEN

A wash-out ahead
so the train stopped for four days
on the prairie near Gleichen.
We played cards, told stories,
dined in Frogmore and St. Cloud.
Silverware, linen and china
chattered in our hands.
Like a picnic some said.

Then the Indians came,
Blackfoot, with their horses.
One dollar, their fingers sang, to ride
across the prairie and lick the sun.
Teeth glinted with sky.
But one pony fell in a badger hole
and broke its neck.
Look, said the man from Detroit,
the Indians will eat it.
They eat anything, diseased and
unclean things. Fingers pointed like
sticks of candy, laughter slapped.
The Blackfoot watched us, eyes bewildered
by sun. They rustled dry grass, vanished
into the yellow land smudge.

The gray horse bloated before us.

Walter Hildebrandt

BROOKS AQUEDUCT

The Bassano Dam
      earthen and hollow reinforced concrete structure
      raised the Bow River
      forty feet
           to carry water
           across a shallow
                two mile
                    valley
first to use the
           hydrostatic catenary curve
        assumed the shape
           of a perfectly flexible container
           holding
                a flowing
                    body
                      of water

boys
                rode their ponies
    to the flume
                on hot summer days
        and cooled off
under the water
        spilling over
the side

        leaking from
           cracks
      cool and shady
                  wet
               trickling
                     down

John Barton

THIS SIDE OF THE BORDER

Alberta lies mostly on the interior plain,
its southern reaches dry
and treeless, flat to the untrained eye.
Outsiders drive quickly west,
seldom notice sloughs far
beneath skies of geese.
They pull off the Trans-Canada
at Brooks, picnic in the irrigated gardens
of the Experimental Farm.
A boy tips up a newly
opened rose.
                    He breathes it in,
the scent vivid as the prairie winds.
He returns to the car, the rose
unlike him bred to withstand
the embrace of winter.

At the edge of each city, before
the poplar groves are ploughed under,
these green oases are rank with children.
Only these trees are old enough
to hold a child, shoulder
forts dreamt about in the school library,
the boards lifted from a half-finished house.
Unwanted jackets hung on lower
branches are thick with dust,
sunset sweating in the wind,
the call home for dinner
virulent as pollen ....

Tim Lilburn

NOW, LIFTED, NOW

I am in the boat of John Cassian's mouth,
        night-coloured, mind-steered, poplar-scented, aspen-lit
ship, old limestone boat, dead ferns pressed into its side. This must
be kept a complete secret, hide it in the fat of your upper right arm.
We are running out of Egypt, holding fire, in paradiso,
burning locks of grass, great in the current, green there, the current a
hump of an animal beneath us, running us out of Africa.
        But soon he leaves me and I am passing through a rabbit scrub place,
antelope field, Bow Valley east of Hays, north of the
confluence with the Oldman, lower jaw valley, the bone of it, the lying-
out-in-the-open of it, eight or nine feet up
in the uttered boat, ribcage anchor dragging along the tops of the grass
showing above snow, storm purpling in, the No. 1 highway starting to
                                            close, the end
of the will in these parts, just long grain trucks dundering through in
                                            heavy snow.

And this place is in the stomach of the thing,
and it is low in the breath.
The eyes in the willow, this willow,
        open ....

Jan Zwicky

HIGHWAY 879

North out of the Sweetgrass Hills, their mass
fixed and improbable in my rearview mirror
the better part of an hour. Sunday,
near-record heat in April, he is asleep
beside me in the front seat.
The air is hazy with evaporating ice, still
you can see for thirty miles:
sheds, dugouts, the gridlock
of stubble and summerfallow, windbreaks
paralleling the section lines, and the road
like some edict of connection,
empty.

      Until
that coulee – the highway
dipping for a moment into olive-velvet shadow
and emerging
changed: the way two people
exhausted by a hard winter can make love
in the late afternoon and wake
to find the clutter of their lives no more than
a few already-leaning fenceposts under wind.
It is that easy to be happy.
Or unhappy. Vastness itself
a singularity.

Monty Reid

WRITING-ON-STONE

> *Haunted places are the only ones people can live in.*
> — Michel de Certeau

i

The landscape is not made into this, it is unmade, flutes of wind, a
substitution of water, reduce it, its signatures reduce it, and then
there is room for the ghosts to inhabit it

                           and altho you may entertain the
thought, out of courtesy or rational self-interest, that there are no
ghosts, there is a space for them, here in the valley's cavity, the
ribs rising on either side, the skin fallen away
                          into which we spill, thinking we
are too light, too permeable to even be real, but in the arid pod of
this valley we rattle against the walls where the inscriptions tease
us with names, what passes through them,
                the hunts, celebrated births, tawny sandstone
palisade against which the cattle gather

ii

for shade just outside the park boundaries within which,
although it is a protected area there is no greater urge than to place
a name on this stone, soft enough that a broken poplar twig can
scratch it
                and it may have meant something,
somewhere, to have the word inscribed upon the rock
but here it is just a way to undue its surface and let another image of
ourselves out
                paler if more recent, but equally indifferent to
preservation, you can see it echo off the terrain wavering with the
heat and so many subtractions, until it disappears
among the apartmented rock ....

Tim Lilburn

KILL-SITE

... Sandhills in a light, likely daylong rain, looking off
    to the left, grass that's not going anywhere, September – everything walks
toward you; it undresses and comes
                    toward you with its small bright hands
and the downwind smell of your father's mind
and his shoulders in the early summer of 1964;
he's working two jobs, post office, moving company, right
now he's not wearing a shirt, a hundred and forty-five pounds,
but still less under the name of his lower-in-the-throat citizenship,
where he's not saying a thing, living in a cave two-
thirds up a cliff line, how
did he get there, swallows heaving in front of his face, the hole
trench-shovelled into clay sides lifting over the Milk River, north of
the Sweetgrass Hills, cattle clouding off infinitely
to the east, feathers
and bones hung from the string at the mouth of the cave,
pale green feathers smooth out long and speechless from his tailbone.
Things climb out of the elms of their names and themselves
and they come forward, moving their tattooed, Fulani hands.
They smell of your father's voice, his
      one
        black
          suit.

WHAT CAN ANYBODY SEE?

What can anybody see in an area
such as Lethbridge or Medicine Hat
or smaller cowtowns south of that
but still in Alberta?   I'm caught among
the clothing of two wind swept poles   White
cloud sheets smother me and a grey saddle blanket
falls heavy   My memory broods
on the way men hang sweaty horse tack
on lines to air along with aprons   dresses
and little kid's shorts   I shiver to think
how minds at an early age shut tight like gates
I still have bruises from trying to lift wires
over staples   another year and another year
How long can a person live in such dry wind?
What is it that makes fragile fingers strong?

In the yard a child in gritty diapers
puts his fists in his eyes   Everywhere I look
dust rises from pastures where bulls lock horns.

Sid Marty

MEDICINE HAT

One time I went back
in a dry month
But all my friends
were gone
from the tumbleweed town
by the brown river

I cannot put the cycle in reverse
The prairie ground
burns slowly dry
as the petrified hills,
leaves this lonely earth

Forecast in a wavering line
of trees, the town grows closer
in the heat haze

The river flows slowly
Broken by the need
of a bottomless sky

Like the river, like the rain
men learn early of need

Macoun wrote to Sandford Fleming
1873; "bunch grass soon dies out
when pastured, and sage brush
takes its place"

No-one heeded his advice,
Sagebrush is the smell of home

Still this land befriends
gophers, coyotes, prairie owls
and man
All who tunnel
water or sweat
into turf

Still, the sun is puzzled
by all pretexts of a town

For only the moon concedes
the roofs of the prairie

Karen Solie

SUFFIELD

From the base, gunplay of soldiers
practicing to erase history, to cancel
like a stamp how long it takes
to build a person, a house.
Year after year he hears this
over the whine of transports carrying
cattle and pigs to the end of time,
the moans that float behind, one red leaf
in the slipstream, and grows old
in the manner of those who live
beside the highway listening
to the engines pass, his hands
fists with a glass at the centre,
delivering rye in blows to the head and gut.
No one stops.
Anyway, his pumps are nearly dry,
while he seeps bitter
as an alkali slough, as though he had spread
his body with salt and given it up
to wind and hours. Is it fall, again?
There is clamour in the wetlands, goslings
deep in the first season of guns.
All that sits is in need of paint
and the rest goes,
everyone with more miles to the gallon,
hoping to slice a few minutes off the trip.

BONEBED: DINOSAUR PROVINCIAL PARK

Out of the scattered bone
reconstruct a herd. Scapula, femur, horncore.
Pattern. Fragment.

There is nothing complete, except the heat,
even with its age accumulated across the dark miles
just to be absorbed in the softness of this landscape.
All those millions of years just leave us exhausted
and without compelling evidence.
So we break for the afternoon and return later
when the strata is warm as a lived-in body, giving back
the heat captured earlier in its mineral glitter,
just as the bones slowly erode at its surface.

Walk among them. Even their shapes
recollect something organic, something with the
heat of evidence in it. Look how the ribs
lie parallel and imagine a river's parallel flow
pulling them that way. Compare the sizes of a bone
known to occur only once in each animal.
What is it you know, as the indirect past
shuttles through the layered Earth.

And if you came back in the moonlight
with the pallid rock still warm and the great
herd of shadows pausing on its way across what
has been interpreted as a coastal plain you will find
the fleshed-out names easy to say. Reflected
light is the real, insistent light.

Kim Maltman

ICE FISHING CESSFORD LAKE

Often there is that deep blue light that comes
before dawn. Over your face you pull the scarf
and step out from the cramped warmth
of the station wagon, from the stifling scents of bodies, coffee
laced with rum, out onto the lake.
The surface powders as you
tramp across it. Tufts of snow whirl up.
You find an old hole, frozen over,
and begin to chip, the steady heft of the ice hammer
wrenching at the layer of mitts and gloves. After a while
you scoop out all the loose bits, then begin again.
The ice re-formed inside the hole is no more than a day old,
yet you're down a foot at least before it gives out
and the weight of the hammer
yanks your hand down after it into the frigid blue-green water.
You put a dry glove on and drop the lines in.
Standing motionless you feel the wind swirl in from all directions,
and there is no shelter.
The fish pile up without a fight, small
barren perch the color of wet leaves matted under trees in spring.
Along their backs the sharp spines
poke out from the fins. They take the hook deep,
so you have to bare both hands to free them, one
sliding back from the head, pressing
the spines down to avoid the poison on them,
squeezing till the mouth opens. Strange,
in summer you can fish for days
and hardly catch a thing but now they just keep
coming. Soon your hands are numb, you start to catch
a few spines, but it's all so easy, you keep wanting
more, a few more. And it's
cold, you feel it working up your legs.
Along the shore the rushes
poke up stiffly through the ice.
An hour past dawn,
a faint glow straddling the skyline.

MIDDAY, MIDSUMMER

The spider's is the only motion on the prairie;
its speed to the moth amazes. I blink
the sweat from my eyes and lose briefly
the blue gut-wrap around the sun.
Insect-whir increases to a pitch of terror
at the awful fate of their own. Far
below, the Red Deer River flows
into the badlands as it has done
for millennia. And I can almost see
the giant beasts crash to the banks
to feed on the current-swept corpses,
to tear flesh from the grey waters
under this same trembling sun,
slavering, insatiate jaw of heaven.

Where is the quick deer,
descending hawk?
The sky of shooting stars?

My blood is cadenced to the insects' terror
as now the spider stops to stun.

Cecelia Frey

WIND AT OYEN, ALTA.

Day in day out
curls its moans around corners
laps its parched tongue
into crevice of chimney
doorframe
blows hollows in grass
daily I grow thin in its press
evenings vow insanity
set deadlines at dawns
each night dream of madness
the form I will take
I'm not opposed to the
crackling granny who lives
in a shack at the edge of town
sifting earth through
her four brown skirts
Still, I prefer
to slip down this skin across my feet
unzip this spine   snap it away
like wash on a line
be carried light as seed puff

Richard Woollatt

HIGHWAY 9, EAST OF HANNA

Yes – *where life is*:
leaving/returning

Giants pounded
prairie flat
trampled & levelled
horizon to horizon
telegraph poles shoulder
wires without slouching
to vanishing point
shimmering asphalt
the only movement on
this treeless plain
    Palliser came this way
    in the dry season of
    another century
    the drylanders' exodus
    began here
    my family among them

Returning in air-conditioned comfort
of self-contained trailer
past Youngstown & Chinook to Cereal
I wonder why I've come
back to this once desert place
where banks pulled out
       (& never came back)
machinery disappeared
in dirt drifts &
tumbleweeds roamed
    empty fields

Jason Dewinetz

BADLANDS

Not until a Drumheller hotel room do we begin to presume.

Breaking apart the bed table
to hold the window open,
you, wearing purple men's briefs,
        your drink on the sill
        threatened by passing trains,
hold out your hand as an answer
        like those women who,
        lowering their heads,
        allowed or deigned their lovers,
and putting your mouth to my eye
taste sand dust.

A mile west this town does not exist,
the ground swallows it,
holds it beneath a wall of sand a hundred feet deep,
        everything bone under it.

Leaning from the window
yelling at the sign you can't reach,
one hand holding the back of my neck.

We have given up playing cards.

One of us may fall out and
I'm not kidding.

Hawk on the street light
tears the throat out of a field mouse.

We talked about going further,
had another drink
before the heat destroyed
larynx, as though fevered.

Didn't speak of it again.

After the hoodoos east of Rosedale
worn smooth as your hip by wind
we put our clothes back on,
and shaking sand into the heat before we left
    buried our footprints.

Christine Wiesenthal

AVIAN SPECIMEN
  (*at the royal tyrrell museum of paleontology*)

for six maybe seven years
i carried you unfocussed around
inside my head, the outline of your
if a skeleton, barely a
grainy ultrasound, a
comet smudged colossal some
by clumsy thumb

particle cloud
of bird, i wished i could hold
you in my left hand,
this left hand being the lighter
(from long disuse; they frowned
when it started to write)

for what stories you could tell
my atrophied fingers, what about
etymology, evolution, extinction and all
the sweet etceteras of their sciences
limned into your dolomite bed.
what deep predictions
you could spill into the wrinkle
of this one lifeline i've left.
mineral sentiments of centuries
in a six-inch wing span:

these you might deposit in my palm
to warm a blue-veined hand again.
and breathe i swear i would not
against your ribs of chalk; nor
would i disturb the perfect
arc of your neck, your head thrown back,
stone eyes closed as though awaiting
or remembering the rapture of
the blindest kiss. but not for me,
i know, to compose your bones into poem,
you having so long ago unfolded yourself
to death in such senseless
excess detail

six years and my right hand still tries
to trace you, every bitter winter
when the windows splinter and fracture
into hairlines of frost.

Bruce Hunter

SLOW LEARNER

1

the way the kid told me
working for the summer
hometown Standard, Alberta
your basic five elevator
one drugstore no bar town
on a spur line near Drumheller
town foreman got him pruning poplar
gave him enough work
to keep out of trouble
the three days he was gonna be gone
prune em up good, top em off here
pointing somewhere near his belt
three days later the foreman was back
all over town, not a tree
higher than the belt on his pants

2

this winter the kid's working on my crew
we're pruning young cottonwood
which stand about chest high
each tree's got two main stems
might look like two
if you didn't know

he's down on the other end
when i decide to see how he's doing
he's gone and cut down every second stem
figuring the other one was a sucker

we kick snow over the stumps
cut down the other half
so the boss won't ever figure
there was a tree here

for the sake of history i'm hoping
we'll both be gone before the snow

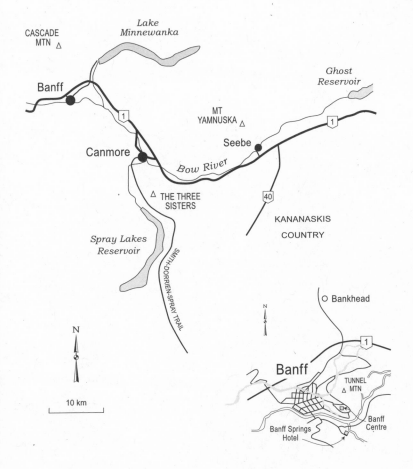

Tom Henihan

BOW VALLEY

An enormous evening
is dying magnificently
over the mountains.
The white skulls of animals
emulate the sky
by flourishing
inside their own dreams
until they are completely lost.
The wind comes and goes
confused as a bird's
first moment of freedom.
The trees waltz
in each others arms
with the ardour of children
at a boisterous wedding.
The river yields to the world
its branches of dark water
while the evening moans
from the depths of its dominion
as it descends the ladder
of its own blood
and enters the clay
that has eaten
the veins of the sky.

TRUST

to fall here
you have to trust
the softness of snow
the enormity of sky

a winter morning in kananaskis
we walked a frozen river-bed
fresh snow over ice
under the ice flowing water
clear in the shade
green under sunlight

we stood still
our heavy boots silenced
listened to the soft trickle beneath
visible winter breath
the river's half hibernation

back at the hotel
so many layers
to unzip, unbutton, untie, unhook, unclasp, pull over
we collapsed
undone down our middles like cut fruit
bits of styrofoam –
that stippled ceiling –
snowed down on us
found the folds of our skins

Erin Mouré

SEEBE

The mind's assumptive power
The assumptive power of the mind over the mind
The carrying of spit upward to the mouth on the end of a knife
this incredible spillage,

release of the river behind the dam at Seebe, recoil of water
rushing the gorge, where we have stood, our lines
taut connection between us & the water's surface, our blastular memory,
(t)autological

who we are, now, the spaces between words where time leaks out
& we are finished, finished, gone old;
the table of food finished & the guests left, & the spillage of glasses, &
our shirts empty, empty,

They say what saves the bones is weight-bearing exercise
except for the carrying of children
Which is our namesake,
which is what we do, naming

children,
taking their torsos in & out of the uterine wall
then carrying them, lifting
the weight of the small boy up from the side of the rails
& running forward to the train, stopped for us, his leg soft with blood
spattered my uniform, his leg not broken, just torn a bit at the skin,

This spillage, rusted gates pulled upward
to release the downstream blood
The mind's assumptive power of the Bow at Seebe
Carrying the boy to the conductor & then running back for the
kit, sunlit, "we hit a cow" they said in the lounge car afterward,
& me lifting the boy up from the dam where he was fishing,
the bridge where the whitefish run among the planted trout at Seebe

lifting him upward, his Stoney Indian face & bone weariness, watching me
white woman from the train taking him upward
into the vast, vast emptiness

Actually he was in the weeds
Actually he was nested hurt leg red in the weeds beside the train
so as not to be found again, got that?
All the tourists on the dam fishing sunlit maybe first hot weekend of
summer, delirium, delirium, trout dreams of the uterine memory, pulled
upward on the thin lines, water running high into the reservoir, oh Bow,
oh hotness,

we hit a cow, they said ....

Kim Maltman

YAMNUSKA

As far as anyone could tell
it sprang full-formed from the summit,
cascaded down upland valleys
and leached the last traces
of fireweed and Indian slipper
from alpine meadows.
It flexed and twisted over deadfall,
wrestled with the scree
that languished where the slope was,
tentatively,
less than perpendicular,
and dusted the rim wall with powder.
And of every million or so grains that fell
was one just more symmetric,
marginally more perfect than the rest,
that slalomed down toward the lake
and dashed against the shore.

There are some – the hunters and the guides –
who swear it paused then,
as if undecided,
but there was no warning.
As it came
it rumbled, scudding downslope
and the dry leaves crumbled in its grasp.
There was no warning.
And the car was found that day
below Yamnuska.

As far as anyone recalls
it quit as it began.
But there are still nights
in the valley
when the summit seems too close,
and then the hunters and the guides
will look to one another,
as if hearing something unfamiliar,
and insist
that it is nothing
but the wind.

Rosalee van Stelten

THE THREE SISTERS

pearl mist, and lowering sky
whose surging clouds cast pellets
among the placid pools, shattering
grey granite shoulders
three mountains, mirrored there

atop a tenuous pine
raven folds coalblack wing
enthroned, echoing Thunderbird
tracing with wary eye

woman, in morning somnolence
bent beneath carapace
of crimson cloth

PROGRESS

Above Canmore, near the Spray Lakes, I sense
that we have climbed too far, and when we
reach our car below it will be someone
else's life I will be stealing. My father
points at a peak we are both too old to
reach. I forget that bodies weigh
more than the light. On the other
side of the peak, power lines hum.
The town site below us is the world
as we left it. Nestled between mountain ranges
waiting for the mountains to crumble.
This is the one moment in our two lives when
we are comfortable together. Neither of us can hear
how the other's head rings with a fear that
mountains make stronger.

This morning while leaving the city
we passed a field of crows. Their cries could not
penetrate the car's closed windows.
My father told me his life story, year by year
up to the day I was born. I could
sense, then, that we had both covered too
much ground. My foot on the accelerator was
heavy as though its placement determined
the rest of our lives. Now above the
highway, nearly above the trees, I know it's
impossible to find the right distance
between us. Each year we move back towards
our beginnings, when Father and son first
discovered each other. It could rain now
and I wouldn't notice, content to find my
place in this landscape, content to know
dreams are not this strange or complete. My
father wants to find wild animals here, a

squirrel, marmot, coyote: it doesn't
matter. He wants to make it to the top of
the trees before dark, and see the clouds
below him for the first time. I suspect
that he knows his limitations too well. I
blame the wild for keeping us apart, he
too comfortable there, I uncertain and
uneasy about my lack of control of it. I
suspect that inside, both of us stopped
looking for our story. It is here above the
highway, animals out of view, the city
forgotten like a dream upon waking.

Colin Morton

AT BANKHEAD
   (*a coalmining ghost town
       near Banff*)

   I
This granite staircase
without its proud manor
stands alone between snow peaks

last witness to these
black wounds
inflicted on the mountain

   II
Follow this cold stream
down till the current
slackens and
sinks
beneath stone

found again
in a coalpit
exposed to the sun
filling with mud and flowers

   III
For fear this black earth
rots on contact
we make love standing

then scramble back to the road
stopping only at the cenotaph
to read the names of the dead

Ian Adam

TRIP TO BANFF

1 Passage

I really wanted to go after all
to see the haystacks like heads blond in the field
the purple mountains devour the sky as we plunge
down Morley Hill,
those four horses drinking at the slough,
the peak scalped by logging, its skull covered with toothpicks,
the spruce dusted white by the cement plant,
the planed violated side of the limestone mountain
and the wind-gusty passage to the Bow valley,

where things start to be as they should be
where hackers and slashers are banned,
where everything is where it should be,
see, the mountains are in place
uniformed in green and hatted with snow
the elk has appeared on cue
bear make their plodding rounds,
lodgepoles dart to a silky sky
late flowers warming at their base,
the chipmunks are waiting on the logs at Sundance:
Banff, you are a postcard whose time has come.

2 Image

but as we pose for photographs
you in imperial view of the valley from the Tunnel Mountain road,
me surveying the golf course just past the Bow Falls froth,
a disturbance touches me   our smooth journey is ruffled
I am looking for a sign   but always return to images,
photographs and postcards
those cute cubs   or cuter Mount Rundle
Kodaked in colour,
or even marvelous early Byron Harmon compositions
his fine-grained black and whites
with their joyous human figures   meticulously scaled
all part of our codes of possession,
our human intrusion
whether back-packing bulky '20's equipment   amazing the places
or zooming the lens of Minolta SLR's
our guided missiles of the image age.

buzzing and clicking away the wilderness
we have joined the others   we are the others
the congested world seeking relief
the walks of the town a jostle of tourists
the streets peristaltic with cars,
gangs at the Cave or on top of Sulphur,
big of Mac or Inuit art gone tack
candy of rock and tartan of Scot
souvenir cluttered shops and Japanese –
where can I find a sign from these? ....

Margaret Avison

BANFF

The skiers dwindle up out of the valley.
The deft wind skims the snow
and with a sudden shift of temper
snarls and snaps at the puffy twigs
    spilling their whiteness on the blue-white drifts
        in patterns pencil-blue.
The long pines lean into the sky. Chalk-blue
the blank sky stares. Anthracite hill
    is blazing white on Tunnel's further flank
and Cascade blazing keen into the sun,
and white spume curls, clenches the green-blue Bow,
    the milk-green, solid-gliding, weltered Bow …
Savage hauteur, accepting cyclic Time
as but the lidding of a frozen Eye …

Gordon Burles

REUNION

Outside my window
September thunder cracks
while inside I drink tea
and talk with you.
Yesterday, an hour after
you arrived, an aspen
drowsily dropped
a crowd of leaves
around my gate, and
I did not disturb one leaf.
Two loves – you and
the fair-haired autumn –
had come back to me.

Today we walked
the high ridges
with cirrus turning cartwheels
and the larch forest,
that golden animal,
ranging on the mountain's back.
A pleasant day, no doubt,
but I felt
the bleak heart of Nature.
The ancient ground,
if you listen,
echoes a myriad goodbyes.
Today I listened
but you pulled me back,
for in your eyes
were imaginings
yearning to be true.
Descending in the dusk
I felt the shadows
pull at me, calling me

toward a forest
dark with lost loves,
the false glory
of self-crucifixion.
When the shadows fled
to infinity
I clamoured after them
till, sage and bitter,
wind stirred the leaves
with memories of
barren broodings
that neither smiles nor tears
could appease: and
I turned hopefully
and embraced you.

Cyril Dabydeen

BY LAKE MINNEWANKA
(*Banff National Park*)

I

We're feeding mountain sheep
(Or goats); what does it matter?
We're asking them to be good citizens –
Or simply to be at their best, while
Rolf, with camera in hand, zooms in,
The lens saying, "Get the horny one."
With aldermanic zest, he's also priest-like:
Lips throbbing over the aesthetic
Quest upon this natural scene
Here in highland Alberta, Lake Placid
Mirroring a semblance of lust or
Lofty pleasure.

And Diane and I are feeding the sheep
Chocolates. "Sure thing, get the horny one,"
Rolf says. "Feed them nuts as well."
From inside the car, images distort
Calgary's distant yet concrete spread.

II

The sheep take off after a while
And politicians like truants
Hurl themselves into the nearby brush
To start hiking, leaving me to mull
Upon the lake's crest, while other
Visitors come by from time to time;
I am now the silent hunter, a grove
All around; jackpine with hooves suggesting
Imminence of danger far away from Ottawa.

III

Suddenly a dog appears, taking after the sheep:
A dozen of them at once; and the Native
Coming out of his camper (his girlfriend close by),
laughs with distorted pleasure as the dog
Snarls: such ferocity in hot weather –
The sheep plunge deeper into danger!
It's what's left now, the vehement strides
With blood flowing, wool and flesh scraped
From bone, all the horny ones really, desire
Still making us survive in the wilderness
Where "nature red in tooth and claw" assures
Of yet another life, if by-laws or fiercer love
By politicians, hardbooted and crushing leaves –
Will less dramatically allow.

Lorne Daniel

WINTER AT THE BANFF SCHOOL

I have been here many days
waiting
expecting something to happen
watching
           : tons of rock
unnaturally on edge
stone seams standing in the air
at the angle of repose
           : the snow
piling wet and heavy onto ledges
and evergreen limbs
From the window in this dark winter
room I see
           : Sue
nine months pregnant
tomorrow   her long blue gown framed
in the window across the courtyard
           : a deer
climbing the slope
from the river   uncertain
of this light that is not moonlight
Across the snow   Sue watches
the doe   I think
of Sue's child and my son
back home and the fawn that may be
waiting
up the mountain

I am searching
for the voice that will speak
for all of us
but the doe and Sue
are moving
slowly
      silently
           away
from the moment
      : the doe
steps into the swirls of snow
cautiously
but is suddenly gone
her tracks blown over
      : Sue's room
across the way
is dark
I stare into snow
that falls steadily   piles heavy
heavier on stretching   bending limbs

waiting

Richard Hornsey

THE ROCKY MOUNTAIN SUMMER MOVIE

The July tourists at Banff
mill among the ski shops
looking at packboards and hiking boots
The Grizzly Bear pizza house
does booming business below Cascade mountain
while fat ladies hurrying back
to their hotel rooms for a shower
are jostled curbward by teenagers
dressed up in smoky leather and denim

A sparkling Vistacruiser from Texas
ticks around the corner
with clouds and restaurant signs
reflected in its tinted windows

Everyone gets a piece of the action
Some scenery framed in a viewfinder
A breath of pine from the motel balcony
Moonlight through a camper screen

A father tells his son
that the animal walking beside the road is lucky
because trappers no longer hang
meat bated with hooks from tree limbs
to catch wolves and martens

But most of all it is the mountains
that are zoomed in upon
Their vast presence broods about the town
like a sleeping beast
which may awaken at any moment
Anticipating the magnitude of disaster
brave vacationers await the twitch

One can be intimate with the force
of mountains   almost casual
Up north in Jasper
far below the lip of Maligne Canyon

where the class of '71 has written
its signature in orange spray paint
a young girl and her companion
fell to their death this afternoon
adding greatly to the attraction

HEAT NEAR BANFF

Ninety degrees
in the shade.
The lodge-pole pines
become tall sticks
of dynamite,
their fuses lengthening
toward the sparking sun.
In this potentiality
of heat
they are about to explode
and blow
their needle shrapnel
out and out
over these hills
and simmering valleys.
Their bursts will scream
out toward my eyes
and heart,
will tear my flesh away.
I dream of running
from these charged trees
but am held fast,
tied tight
in ropes
of smoldering resin.

Sid Marty

THE SAND PILE

Ice falls on Cascade Mountain
from a cornice on the east face
down a couloir, into the mile wide cirque
The blocks come tearing, the impact
booms across the valley like artillery fire

Two miles below, my son looks up
from his sandpile, where he tumbles
kernels down a heap of dust

He's terrified a colony of ants
They flee before his fingers
Scurrying motes of rust

Erin Mouré

CARDIAC GRIZZLIES

At Banff this summer, the river lunged steeply at us,
ungainly beings picking our bodies across the rocks,
balanced incredibly on the cliff above.
Or alone
the three os us hulked over coffee in the Praha
working our way thru the mood
of each other, the speeches.

Sooner or later the rain falls out of its cupboards
& cries.
Ratty wet sparrows in their summer clothes
pick the earth up in their beaks;
when they shake it out
their heads tremble wildly among the cars.
We sit on the furniture in the rented rooms, three
cardiac grizzlies with our huge heads,
the hair painstakingly combed,
the human   well-learned, tho
our talk sounds like leaves that talk
to leaves, on the dark side of the tree.

Our own wildness by the river, outpouring our own banks too,
the feeling of this tangled getting-together
twice a year, not enough
by a long shot but
better than staying alone, in the rough den of our cardiac lives
on two sides of the Rockies.
It's us,   the crazy silent pawing ones, the ones
that crash thru underbrush to keep myths alive,   capable of
finding each other when we need to,
in uncertain territory.
Capable of sustenance & love.

Charles Noble

BANFF: SPACE/TIME SWINDLE

Land tricks are mountains
which show end's meaning
in the middle
horizons we can touch
closeness gotten out of hand.

Disorderly hard shapes
impervious to much direct use
caught napping by
those who think young
and uselessness something to be
gotten away with.
Haven accidentally preserving
a lower spread of life
scientifically touched
with immediate results
these small and larger
furry gods
preying on newspapers

a sensible ground
for the given

teeming world of nature
up to date unhistorical
free and open church
whose altars change
the sleep edges
to quick tastes
of experimental rats
the causally unneedy
losers of miraculous need

where need is flattened to money
and wonderfully useless unproperty
is seen as merely priceless
and frustration is shy of meaning

here consumerism sharpens
to the swivel man
pure and simple
and a good time has been had.

Ruth Roach Pierson

UP TUNNEL MOUNTAIN TRAIL

Laboured, breathless, sweaty. Exposed
roots like ropey veins on the back
of ageing hands. I pause to pant. Up ahead
something small flitters and I see
a chipmunk stand up, strum the Pei Pa. Sun
spangles the drugget of frost on pine needles
scattered like the pick-up-sticks of childhood.
Where do we get the notion that everything
will be all right in the end? Grey flakes of bark
cling to the trunk of the dead, still standing tree
I lean into, feel the brittle, rough rind,
wonder at the will to hold on, how my father
denied anything was wrong, tried to swim
a dozen laps though he'd twice choked
with that dread croaking sound. At the summit
I breathe out into the encircling peaks three huge
OMS echoed by trucks crossing the valley
out of which I've climbed, while in my feet
I feel the start of the slip, the tumble
down the mountain face, hands clutching
at roots, rocks,
straws.

Christopher Wiseman

IN THE BANFF SPRINGS HOTEL

Their furniture is still here –
the dusty high-backed chairs, old
Mahogany desks for letters home,
Brocade covers, velvet curtains –

And it is easy to see them sitting,
Horses stabled by willing grooms,
Mountain clothes unpacked, laid out,
Ready for a bracing promenade,

Or with plummy voices ordering
Pink gins before dinner, maids
Wisping past in black dresses
And starched aprons, waiters gliding,

Deferential, well-tipped, in awe
Of such intrepid wanderers
Of Empire revelling in their history,
What tales to tell of mountains and bears!

And it's still their place. Their ghosts
Sit with rugs over their knees
Looking up the valley. The red
Of the map brought them all this way

To take the healing waters, or see
The real sublime before they died.
Some came to find needed remoteness
Or ease creaking bones. No matter why.

To dream of building this out here,
So far from anything, and then
Transform it into magnificence,
Shows they were special in their way,

That it's too easy to dismiss them,
Those parodies with white moustaches,
Pale ladies in silk and muslin, butlers,
Maids, world-labelled steamer-trunks,

Their tough proud ridiculousness.
Today diminishment – loud kids,
Jeans, cheap trinkets, banks of video-games –
And I surprise an anger in myself,

A fierce desire for stylishness,
And I feel, from the wide terraces,
From card-tables and smoking-rooms,
Flushed, braying, their ghosts approve.

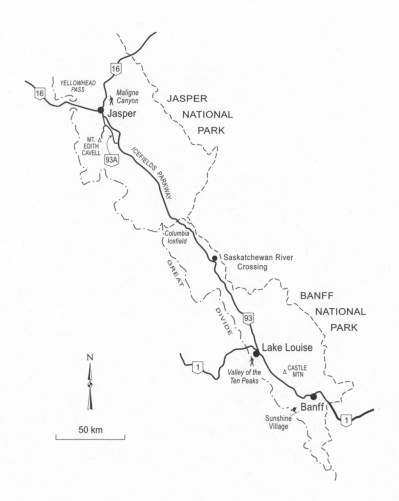

16 YELLOWHEAD PASS

16

Maligne Canyon

Jasper

MT. EDITH CAVELL

93A

ICEFIELDS PARKWAY

JASPER NATIONAL PARK

Columbia Icefield

GREAT DIVIDE

Saskatchewan River Crossing

BANFF NATIONAL PARK

93

Lake Louise

1

Valley of the Ten Peaks

CASTLE MTN

Banff

Sunshine Village

1

N

50 km

Fiona Lam

DEPARTURE
(*Highway to Lake Louise*)

Everyone is leaving.
The night is pushing day down into the ground,
pelting rain as hard as it can at everything
it can hit, beating us
into landscape. The road curves up
under the clenched speed of the little Mazda
that you will one day take from me.

The car shudders in the wake of fleets
of two tonne trucks and moving vans.
Mountains submerge us
as we ascend into Alberta,
a place where coastline and home
don't exist. At this speed,
you maneuvre your words just like your turns,
in tense, quick jerks of the wheel,
yanking us further away
from whatever I felt for you.

Everyone is leaving.
I am pushed
against the door with each twist
of your hands and the road,
but, I ensure, never against you,
just against what at any time
might jolt open, might break
free.

Jim Green

POWER LINE TO SUNSHINE

catch it
catch it in your hands
catch it
catch it while it rides
open wide the door
and in it slides

dry rustling aspen leaves
purring creek water sounds
dawn people
gliding in across the floor

sunrise
morning in the mountains
stars fading from the pink
splash of scarlet
dawn riders ....

Vanna Tessier

STONE JACK

hiking with 3 friends
atop Castle Mountain
wind whistling in their ears
a call from above
        see him
        count his blessing
        carved on rough-edged rock
couldn't get away with it
2 of his friends stop midway
Jack breathes in sky
& stomps on the steep slope
daring to take a solo picture up there
a prohibited pledge
pewter body captured at the edge
on a rock-strewn mountain

poses for his picture
on a ledge
but stones break loose
under his feet
rolls 200 metres
down the mountainside
      his friend runs 4 miles
couldn't find any help
    Jack's lasting
impression on stone
remains
untouched

WENKCHEMNA

… Bright-wedged, glacier-studded, buttressed peaks in serried rank
  surround the lake, retreat in height apparently as they withdraw.
  Talus cones from the cols' long chutes
  heap leaden-brown, streaked with arctic willows,
  decaying roots and rotting leaves forming
  the dun of striving soil;
  if there be colour here,
  the lake reveals green in blue as wind riffles shot silk,
  fracturing sky, the arrows the lake's reflection forms,
  indexes signifying other points:
  spruces thrusting fingers at the sky,
  the drawn-in swoop of valley scoop the glaciers   carved   directing mind,
  the 3-4-5s' triangularity forms gnomons of the peaks,
  the past of Eozoic ooze, Late Cambrian exoskeletons discarded,
  the Pleistocene's devouring too of what lived here

to form what's here ….   ·

Jon Whyte

WRITING THE MOUNTAINS: BANFF TO JASPER

MIND OVER MOUNTAINS

lake	:	lake bottom	::	|	:	reflection
(suggestions		(of syllogism				endlessly) reflecting)

	::	brow	:	mind
	::	broken bowl	:	rim
	::	form	:	idea
	::	substance	:	essence
	::	world	:	cosmos
	::	a life	:	a history
	::	a moment	:	eternity
	::	personality	:	humanity

each   analogy   explicating   implicit   analogues   of   surface:

child's mind,   innocence in nature,   the feral and ferocious; so:

five years old,
growing in a sense of tininess
mountains ceasing to be *skena*, the zenith *proskena*

backdrop

Was it then?   At Lake Louise?

(*not the postcard Lake Louise, but the place I had not yet been to, seen*)

143

GREAT DIVIDE

There,
on the
edge
of
consciousness.

That
imaginary
line,

which sends our
thoughts
to one
coast
or the
other.

Great the effort
to straddle
the physical
barriers
and release

the mind,

know the freedom
of unity

with the divine.

Tammy Armstrong

COLUMBIA ICE FIELD

Stretched like a jagged scab,
this field of muck and rock separates past from present.
Unprepared in summer dress
for an ashen island of sheet ice,
I shiver before a disposable camera eye –
hot coffee offered on the other side of the highway.

Clad in Gore-Tex, you stand several yards away,
fibreglass marker at your feet –
the space your ten-year-old body had occupied in '71.
It's moved so far since I was small.

Chilled, I wait for you to seal this onto a gummy page
in your pocketbook consciousness,
wait over a slough of candy wrappers and cigarette filters,
empty film cartridges strewn like spent bullet shells –
all crunched under the sneakers of children in bright raincoats.

SASKATCHEWAN CROSSING CAFÉ

Mountains are unmoved by music
everything that money can buy
fails, where they lean in the window

I got spurs
that jingle
              jangle
        jingle

but broke them on stones

I work around here
but everything I blast
or smash
is healed by running water

Moss grows back
like a green flesh
Tree stumps rot
and disappear

The jangling steel guitar
the radio bonging away
are stifled out there
in the sound
of falling water
falling ice
falling rock
falling snow

And the music
breaks down

Douglas Barbour

IN MALIGNE CANYON:
  for Marguerite & David Schleich:

1

the water   falls
deep & shallow,   the white
water falls sideways in shadow & out
streams by   a horizontal storm
we dream in /
                    what do we see?

we dream / we see

nothing

of importance,   all importance gone
all import lost in the surge of
white & green we begin to lose   sight of
our selves   lose
nothing we want to keep,   nothing
we need,   nothing
at all really:

            nothing

which we see in the water
as it falls   rush of white
& falls   rippled green window
& falls
        & falls
                by our open wide eyes

2
the rock
walls of the canyon
are carved
in many strange designs
the lines of strata shine
in the bright sun / water
            swirling below

the rock is carved
by water
            (by time)

a process   so far from
art   our delight
has no antecedents in
meaning/

            (no reference
in a form: no 'form')

the rock is
there,   the water
does not stand still

            it moves for centuries until

the rock is carved

            again/

the rock is carved.

3

there is no pain
in canyons   as they
slowly form,   no suffering?

we say this   but
we cannot know.

i speak of slow pain
the erosion of a nerve takes centuries
& the pain,   the pain I say
is slow/

    rock pain
it grows with loss
as all pain grows

    & somewhere

a silt of pain
less sand   builds up

a delta

& i know the pain is slow
there for it waits
     as always

pain/

it waits to grow .

4
mere humans
we walk fast across the bridges
down the trails
                    slow
but still fast
as we stumble up again

& breathe fresh air we need
to climb the hill,   the canyon
walls dont move at all

the canyon walls are rock
paintings of tremendous time
's long torture of the earth's sweet flesh

that man & earth can bear
because so 'natural,'   so very
slow/

        a hole this deep
emerges in a microsecond
/light that blinds,   & heat
removes the flesh of man
& earth below

                    : machined,
the swift & stupid wound,
the kill.

                the kill
is worse than pain
however slow,   it can

deposit nothing elsewhere
for there's nowhere else to go.

5
here
in this natural
place & its proper
movement

through time & space
the seasons come
& go,   the water flows
snow & ice work
wonders on the rock
we walk on now in summer sun
& heat

& i see you ahead
above / below
you move with grace
'willowy' i think/
                    to go
beyond cliché to nature's
own pure image: how you
weave a willow's slow dance
through these trees   across
this rock

i watch all this
seeing far beyond the moment   but
you pull me back to
'this place'   'this time'

& i walk on with
you, new
each moment
in my arms around you
each moment
i choose to hold you   so .

David McFadden

MOUNTAIN AIR

"Now is the time for poets, if they must think,
to think about the future."

Hoping to prop his shrunken ego
some pompous professor yelled this out
at the foot of Mount Edith Cavell
as if by stressing his self-importance
the mountains would come alive
and he caught his shrunken echo.

How long have these mountains
been young? So long that if you fell now
you'd never stop falling
and you'd never stop screaming
and if you could ever really know
your body would collapse like the bodies
found in five graves at Golden Mycenae
by Schliemann who said *I have gazed
on the face of Agamemnon*

and a large fatherly hand
comes out of the sky
and touches the earth like a bowling ball

and if you look through these binoculars
you'll see tiny mountain goats climbing
his knuckles.

I can't help it.

II

To write involuntarily
as mountains are formed
as ice grows on the peaks

as forests clothe the slopes
directly
            instead of only after
hasty study of the proper methods
of producing work merely mimetic
of the involuntary mind

something will not let a mountain err

the stone came to rest
here not there
and I pick it up
and throw it there

it's still the same stone
but if that mountain were here
it wouldn't be the same mountain
unless it suddenly moved
miraculously whether voluntarily
or not

the mind views ultimate horror
in a darkened theatre

I can write compassion
cannot be forced but it can

a curious cloud clings to the peak
some grand stillness on the surface
of a madly spinning world
and on TV an important voice says
make one move closer to simplicity
and I'll fill you full of lead.

And it happens all the time.

Even at the time of the formation
of these mountains with one mountain
falling on another over and over

there was no disturbance.

Perhaps occasional laughter
from the depths.

Doug Beardsley

JASPER BEARS

If I told you how many times I dreamed
we would be like this; two Jasper bears
waltzing down the highway, birches
reflecting themselves in the silver

ice of the sun, you would not believe me,
you would speak of the shape of things:
ridges, gradations, rose-light on Mt. Robson,
your fingers revealing the tip of each peak.

Coming down the canyon, ice at the edge,
the thick emerald water, we share
the first winter, carry it and come through.
What mountains are more beautiful

than your almond eyes, your olive skin.
Yours is the hand I wish to hold, your
honeyed fragrance always on my flesh.
Everything I've seen till now I've missed.

Take me love, teach me all over again,
the way you want to be touched.

A REASON

Driving fast in March
through the high, cold valley of the Athabaska
past Jasper,
I see men
lying out on the ice.

This lake has four or five men
bundled in sleeping bags
atop air mattresses or foam.
They lie face down, as though staring into the ice.
The next lake has two, with one man standing between them
whose eyes follow the cars as we speed
by a couple of pickups parked
just off the highway.

But the figures out on the ice
continue to lie face down.

Beyond the lakes, the mountains
are a stone backdrop in the sunshine.
And I think:
there is a reason
these men are here – fishing, perhaps,
though there are no poles or tackle boxes visible
and why they have to remain
looking into the ice
I can't guess. But then
what do I understand of these mountains
– their shapes familiar from the highway,
or a summertime hike in a safe corner?
The road, on the other hand, I am sure of
but what do I know about how asphalt is made
or how to set the timing on this car?

And yet I drive
staring over the steering wheel at the Rockies

and at men lying motionless
on the frozen water.

YELLOWHEAD

What's written is little, so argues me a fragment
of the past, fair haired trapper of the smoky peaks
gave my name to the famous pass, and Tete Jaune Cache
I had a name once, now I am Yellowhead

Now that I'm a place and not a man
my faults are forgotten, why should I remind you

History magnifies everything

Like others, I was all flash and fire once
a young buck in tight breeches
My head was an emblem, and protean
I managed to keep it on my shoulders
No mean feat in the times I lived in

I tell you this
It was a hard life

So you built your highway
and stole my emblem
my brave belt don't fit you
so bask in secondhand magic
and buy off the dead as long as you can

I could not keep a secret
keep my power hidden

Everywhere I went they knew me
a bright flame
moving through purple shadows

They said   it is Tete Jaune
it is Yellowhead,

Yellowhead

7

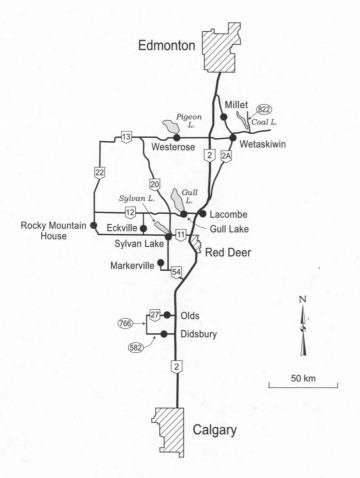

Edmonton

Millet

822

Pigeon L.

Coal L.

13

Westerose

Wetaskiwin

2   2A

22

20

Sylvan L.

Gull L.

12

Rocky Mountain House

Eckville

Lacombe

Gull Lake

11

Sylvan Lake

Red Deer

Markerville

54

27

Olds

766

Didsbury

582

2

N

50 km

Rosalee van Stelten

DIDSBURY AUCTION

Right off the range, she was
tawny Charolais heifer
never before saw halter, heard
triple-tongued auctioneer

Straight from the city, was I
drugstore cowgirl, tooled
leather boots never tested
steel of the stirrup, stepped
in the stream of manure

Didsbury auction stand:
eight-foot counter, windows
behind, swinging gate
on the right, three steps down
to sawdust sprinkled floor

Brown eyes crazed
the heifer bolted, leaped
on the left to the stand

Glass shattered
Blood spattered
She charged

I kicked, swung, hung
on the gate above the arena
Horns and hide grazed my side
hooves clipped my spine

Off in the corner, she snorted
and pawed; the crowd roared
to its feet. *Is this how a cowboy feels
gored by a bull?*

Finally, they led her away
terrified Charolais, and I
cowed, swung back
for my last stand.

Tim Bowling

CEMETERY AT OLDS
  (*en route to the Rockies for the weekend*)

Late, we missed the highway turnoff to earth's more obvious beauty,
dragging the last light with us in a winding-sheet of dusk, to come upon
this lesser range, low peaks quarried from our mortal loss –
how long? a hundred years? Slowing, we shouldered close
enough to feel the utter blackness of the tombs, the weight
of the lowbranched windbreak-forest pressing down to buff the names –
no room for any but evergreen mourners, no room
for even the wind to wreathe the headboards of all sleep.

Three friends, and young, we'd driven half-a-mile past
the proper roadmap mark, to learn that all anarchic laughter
ends in awe of endings. Soon the night was shovelled
silent on our hood and roof. And flakes of snow began
to fall, as if in counterpoint to darkness, or
like missing dots that seek to join their dominoes
slow-toppling in this foothill calm, leaning, but never touching,
pushed by something ancient, starlight or grief, a long game
under the hard wood, played without us, but because of us,
because we hew remembrance from and for the ache of life.

Suddenly, but together,
shivering for the brevity of touch,
we burned our bones like so much paper
in the ashen air between the stones.

Alice Major

NEAR RED DEER
   (*from* Landscapes)

This land is vain and knows she is courted
                  for her wealth.
She lets grain trickle between the long fingers
left by labouring swathers
and lets rivers run slowly down her thighs.

She fingers cloth-of-gold and the embroidery
of wheat fields
colours her lips with saskatoon berries,
smiles seduction upwards at the sky.

Stephan G. Stephansson

MY REGION

Plains of gleam, palace of hills,
blue slopes and rocky mountains
chiselled with valleys and tributaries.
Aspen mound, the river blue,
pastureland, peat marsh,
groves in the crusted range.

Ascend in the west
midway above the plains
sun patches of vivid blue heights.
Gladweather grown calm
flushes through summer woods,
warm creeks thread the valley.

High up mountain crags
arise and all flash
restless in morning's mirage.
Unclouded eastern sun
blazes up glen and grade,
reddens the granite cliff's glaze.

My brilliant-faced region,
when sun beams warmest
it is good to walk alone with you.

A new thought laughs to me,
silently that awakens in
every glen and rock pillar.

I seem to see the same
appearance and recognize
the dale and domed alpine vault,
that is borne by my mother
Silver white, your sister!
You are still more mature, older.

SEASON OF LEAVING (SYLVAN LAKE, ALBERTA)

1

The season to leave is spring
or possibly fall
Summer holds
as it held my forefathers:
green and tangling
growing back
back where I cut it down
and trimmed its wildness
last year
Winter white challenges
with its assault on activity
of all kinds; snow traps
quickly   quietly
Even now the white weight
hugs the barn
towards the ground

2

In town the buildings are all squat
half-sized and humorous
All winter long the windows
and skin-happy swimmers
have been in hiding
behind boards   terrorized
by stark flat miles of wild ice
On the way   driving down to Sylvan
I can see shades of the Pacific
    dark   warm   and blue
rolling over white-profiled mountains
Soon the seasonal decay begins
again   snow turning brown
winter   an empire gone decadent
and soft

3
I have stopped
in the past   stayed
to add new limbs of life
to old wood
(always wood) frames:
new timbers   squared and strong
forced under the old
nailed into place as saviours
of some sad structure
Lately   though   I've been remembering
long-necked beer bottles
dark and musky
cob-webbed to roughed-in window sills:
I wonder if the lines I build
will stand as long

4
Years ago   David Thompson
axed his way through trees
near here   enroute to
Rocky Mountain House and beyond
Now the Government of Canada
calls in engineers with fine instrumentation
to keep the last
remains of the fort
from washing down
the North Saskatchewan River
Nature keeps doing that:
washing back
downstream
down east
these pretences of civilization

In spring   I find myself
running with the water

MEDITATIONS ON THE IMPROBABLE HISTORY OF A SMALL TOWN
Hate Teacher Convicted Again
July 17, 1994

Midway between Red Deer
and Rocky Mountain House on Highway 11.
Eckville pop. 800
and Jim Keegstra.
Former auto mechanic, former
school teacher, now auto mechanic again.

The original settlers recognizing potential
in the belly above the Bible belt
called it Hell
under their breath.
Grasshoppers, drought,
and mosquitoes
when it finally did rain.

But it's not the kind of name
that goes on a CPR map
in a fine new country.
What about Heck, someone offered.
Too obvious said another.
Someone else: Heckville.
A remittance man
with a sense of humour,
so the township papers came back
Eckville.

What happened here
happens in every small town.
Some born, some died, most
moved away.

Until a man taught history
the way you rebuild engines:
do a bit here,
drop this, add that
and what you don't have
make yourself. Found himself teaching math:
six million equals zero.
No one saw anything,
not the principal nor the school board.

And when the trial's over
and the reporters go back
to Toronto or Calgary or Tel Aviv,
the principal and the superintendent
still there and the name
Eckville.

Although sometimes
it must be Hell.

Gerald Hill

SISTERS OF THE GARDEN

I vacuum under the pulpit
of the Catholic Church in Rocky Mountain House.
The only sound is a vacuum cleaner, a Kirby,
which I jostle against the carvings
of holy figures – they've been carved
and still for more than a hundred years.

The rugs are clean
and pure under the nuns' footsteps
on their way to water
plants upstairs. They're Sisters
of the Garden and silent
as leaves.

And I don't speak or violate
that stained glass light
or dust off any object
which might be a piece of the cross
(like my uncle did
at Notre Dame College in Wilcox, Sask.
The priest gave him *supreme* shit.)

I respect the confessionals
in Rocky Mountain House.
I store the Kirby in one of them
and whisper to it.

Ken Rivard

GULL LAKE ALPHABET

seagulls know when dinner is served.
they drag their shadows over my campsite.
shadows are fat
gulls are not
shadows are fat.

campfire has its own alphabet.
it is teaching me how to read a man
who tells stories about generator trips to South America.
I wonder about gull habits in Lima and Peru.

to my left is an inflated silver cigar
on my right a red and white tin box with windows.
I love the water and absurdity of this place
in the above order of course.

on the road back the morning levels the sky.
to the west a giant Japanese woman is
watching over mountain and bird.
she is holding her grey fan
like a book of too many stories.
she is reading aloud to me
by asking if I like her hair
curled just the way it is.

Monty Reid

THE ALUMNI GAME AT LACOMBE ARENA

Kindopp can't buy a goal.
Breaking in alone and fanning
or ringing a shot off the goalpost
from twenty feet. He chases his
own rebound into the corner
passes it behind the net
and when the puck comes back to him
someone lifts his stick.
When the defenceman walks in and scores
they don't even give Kindopp an assist.

After the game he pulls his skates off
drags the sweater over his head.
I'm getting too old for the game he says
if I had a dime for every chance I had ....
He strips and showers and flicks
the wet towel at his right winger.
It's not til he's half-dressed
and reaching for his comb
that he makes the discovery,
along with the rest of the team,
that someone left the dressingroom open
and his wallet's gone
and that he's not really worried
about the money
but he'd like the i.d. back.

Sally Ito

AT THE REYNOLDS MUSEUM
   Wetaskiwin, Alberta

Beyond the museum of the automobile
and the Aviation Hall of Fame
is a wide field filled with the rusted, hulking frames
of yesterday's machines.

Between the orderly rows of rotting red
are speckles of sheep
blithely grazing
under the rickety spout
of some old combine
or beside the shell
of an old beast
that roared down the highways
belching smoke and steam.

When all our remembering and finger-pointing
is done at the museum,
we can sit outside and watch the sheep
minister to the noble folly of this –
our clunking, rusted age.

COAL LAKE

A half
bottle of
Chianti in
Leduc.
There is not
to be a poem
starting
And if I
could have held you
in my
mind about
the Millet-We-
taski-
win stretch of
old Highway 2.
The point
would have been
non-memory
because
of a lack
of distinction.
But the
gravel roads
turn out to be,
subtly,
lazily,
evocative.
August,
if green, is
a good time to
be back:
the pathos
of not feeling
lets up

in the face
of the farming
the big
sky presses,
squeezing it out,
ground not
figure, lo-
cus of no vis-
ible
stir, no work
yet, just growing.
Coal Lake
Reservoir
now with picnic
tables,
deserted
all afternoon
(Friday),
water blue
intense as leaf
green in-
tense as wind
just moves them both
so the
leaves have a
white to them and
the lake
its ripples –
and the clover
like both
(leaf, flower).
To remember
this may
not be so

hard. Almost to
feel, too.
She would be
glad I have walked
away from
the tables
across the field
(clover)
to where the
berries are, but
not for
them (sparse, sour
here), for distance.

*

A Blue
in a new
Wetaskiwin
place to
eat and drink,
the waitress in
hot pants,
net stockings,
but as wholesome
as we
always were,
while the decor
is an
improvement:
checked table-'cloths,'
posters,
French-flag-toned
hangings, the walls
so hued.

Erin Mouré

WESTEROSE

Walking on Billy's land near Westerose, amid sunken prints of
deer that came
all winter to the spilled barley

Walking in Billy's yellow field
beside the willows, their leaves scented & green;
I walk in the rusty light of evening
toward the spring he talked of.
Behind me, our mother dozes in her car; an hour away
Mary drives Billy toward us
from Edmonton.
Still I am walking his land, fields of my youngest brother.
A tall spirit lodged among furrows, I dream
how   our growing changed us, who grew so closely –
The money & speculation,
the turning-away from each other for years
that ends *here,* as Billy speeds closer down the highway
with his girlfriend Mary,
my own brother, & my long-time friend.

& I think of how the years will shape this family,
beyond the sudden shifts   of perspective & loneliness
that displace us all;
I dream how Billy's land awaits us,
to complete our awe for each other's lives
in its stubble, among tracks of hungry deer

Yet I am afraid of our lives
not working,
of subdivision & profit in land, of arriving
& not finding Mary here, unable   to kiss her,
my new sister;
I fear my hard self becoming a manager in Vancouver,
& my mother with her sad dreaming, shut into the car.

These are fears   of a tall woman aging
as she walks the grey-wooded soil, unplanted yet this year,
scaring   birds out of the old stubble;
I turn toward the road
just as Mary turns her car into the driveway
behind my mother's,
& Billy steps out with her to greet us.
As I come down from my pasts and futures   into their embrace,
to live where I am *now*,
on the slope in the murmur of willows, the gully
creek-noise, with my family and friend near Westerose, in the tough light of
evening, like   deer last winter, meeting on Billy's land.

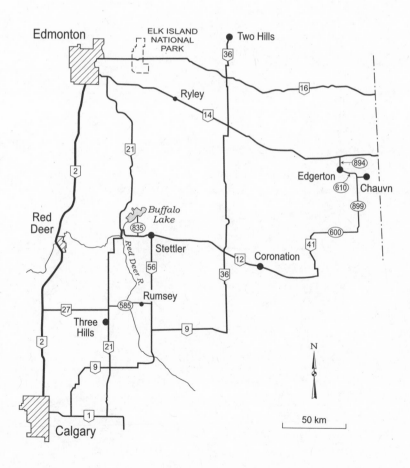

Edmonton

ELK ISLAND
NATIONAL
PARK

Two Hills

36

16

Ryley

14

21

2

894

Edgerton

610

Chauvn

899

Red
Deer

Buffalo
Lake

835

600

41

Stettler

56

Red Deer R.

12

Coronation

36

Rumsey

27

585

9

Three
Hills

2

21

9

N

1

50 km

Calgary

Richard Woollatt

NORTH OF THREE HILLS THE PARKLANDS BEGIN

North of Three Hills
the parklands begin
and rolling northward
on Highway 21
I savour the last
uncluttered
wide-angled view
of the prairie's contours
patterns of crop against crop
    rapeseed yellow
    barley wavering green
    wheat heading out
    pasture browning
rectangles of velvet
undulating in heat & wind
beside the three hills
skipped across the plain
by retreating glaciers –
    round loaves
    halved & settling
    into grain

Prairie recedes
a black ribbon of road
winds me into a rug of farms
poplar bluffs & sloughs
populated by pintails & mallards
jauntily feeding
    tails skyward

each pond a teeming
microscopic world
rivalling hamlet & village
clinging like amoebas
to the map's red line
    Trochu, Huxley, Elnora
    Delburne & Mirror
    on Buffalo Lake
    and I'm home, free
    in parklands again

Bonnie Bishop

THE RUMSEY MORAINE

those hills nest
in a yellow prairie
woven on the edge of a valley
huddled, murmuring
mound after mound after mound
heads under wings

you must see them
if not for their flight pattern
then for their quiet roundness
smooth desire
slipping from the visible
boundary of highway
    you want to lay
    your body close
    a bird in a hand
    or a hand to a breast

Richard Woollatt

NORTH & WEST

Moving from south
of Coronation
east of Hanna
Bennett buggies
democrats
Model T's & A's
Chevrolet trucks
hay racks & grain wagons
radiators steaming
horses' ribs streaming sweat

belongings lashed to
roofs bumpers fenders
or in boxes strapped to
        running boards

in trucks
crates of chickens
squalling pigs
behind wagons
a milk cow with calf

fleeing drought/grasshoppers
hail/tumbleweeds
army worms/sawflies

coming west to Parklands
north to Peace River

188

from Cereal & Chinook
Lanfine   Excel
Esther   Sedalia   Naco
Richdale   Sunnynook
Buffalo & Bindloss
six thousand people
    half the population from
    eight thousand square miles
moving north & west
parchment faces

leaving behind homes
    scorched & shrunken
    dreams
barns
    caragana hedges thick
    with dust
machinery
    (*bought dear sold cheap*)
slough bottoms cracking

Alice Major

SOUTH OF STETTLER
　(*from* Landscapes)

the land collects water in small round candles.

The geometry of lines grooved by swathers
becomes complex, curved, non-Euclidean –
concave reverses into convex.

Round hay bales nestle side by side against a rise
like a row of piglets crowded against teats.

Other hills suckle poplar stands or pines
that stand up to the sky.

Richard Woollatt

ROADS TO BUFFALO LAKE

Hot always hot in Mirror
when we left
ruts at corners of
sandy streets
      sucking narrow wheels down

          but woods were cool as
          sawdust-littered icehouses

white road beckoning us
        over hills bumping
around the buffalo's hump
as we watched for our shining lake
scorched landscape oasis

Old Chevvie bucking to top
of first high hill
revealing
      glint of waves
        on distant sandbars
before woods again
fragrant with balm-of-gilead
weaving through trail mazes
off the main road
seeking Bar Harbour Beach
– but always a wrong turn
      dead end at barn door
      or straw stack
        (for my father loved new trails
        loved fitting wheels into
        cool ruts
        leading over knolls where
        Cree and Metis hunters
        had stalked buffalo
        coming to water)

At each wrong turn we cried
      Where's the lake?
until glimpsing blue
        through screen
        of green poplars
we raced through hot backwater pools
to the cool of waves
curling sandribbed bottom

Robert Kroetsch

SEED CATALOGUE

4

It arrived in winter, the seed catalogue, on a January
day. It came into town on the afternoon train.

Mary Hauck, when she came west from Bruce County, Ontario,
arrived in town on a January day. She brought
along her hope chest.

She was cooking in the Heisler Hotel. The Heisler Hotel
burned down on the night of June 21, 1919. Everything
in between: lost. Everything: an absence

of satin sheets
of embroidered pillow cases
of tea towels and English china
of silver serving spoons.

How do you grow a prairie town?

> The gopher was the model.
> Stand up straight:
> telephone poles
> grain elevators
> church steeples.
> Vanish suddenly: the
> gopher was the model.

How do you grow a past /
to live in

the absence of silkworms
the absence of clay and wattles (whatever the hell
                  they are)   .
the absence of Lord Nelson
the absence of kings and queens
the absence of a bottle opener, and me with a vicious
                  attack of the 26-ounce flu
the absence of both Sartre and Heidegger
the absence of pyramids
the absence of lions
the absence of lutes, violas and xylophones
the absence of a condom dispenser in the Lethbridge Hotel and
                  me about to screw an old Blood whore. I was
                  in love.
the absence of the Parthenon, not to mention the Cathédrale de
                  Chartres
the absence of psychiatrists
the absence of sailing ships
the absence of books, journals, daily newspapers and everything
                  else by the *Free Press Prairie Farmer* and
                  The Western Producer
the absence of gallows (with apologies to Louis Riel)
the absence of goldsmiths
the absence of the girl who said that if the Edmonton Eskimos
                  won the Grey Cup she'd let me kiss her
                  nipples in the foyer of the Palliser Hotel. I
                  don't know where she got to.
the absence of Heraclitus
the absence of the Seine, the Rhine, the Danube, the Tiber and
                  the Thames. Shit, the Battle River ran dry
                  one fall. The Strauss boy could piss across it.
                  He could piss higher on a barn wall than any
                  of us. He could piss right clean over the
                  principal's new car.
the absence of ballet and opera
the absence of Aeneas.

How do you grow a prairie town?

Rebuild the hotel when it burns down. Bigger. Fill it
full of a lot of A-1 Hard Northern bullshitters.

– You ever hear the one about the woman who buried
   her husband with his ass sticking out of the ground
   so that every time she happened to walk by she could
   give it a swift kick?

– Yeh, I heard it.

Bruce Hunter

FOR MY BROTHER DANIEL

"BENCHMARK"

starting point of a survey

driving down from survey school
on highway 41 north of Battle River
miles of uninterrupted bush
save one small graveyard
with its white framed mission
beside it tombstones
high-centered in sweetgrass
these final shapes of ancestry
dust and bones without light
faces in the family album
funeral wreaths of ox-eyed daisy
and yarrow mark their roads

Tim Lilburn

HEARING

Land around Dillberry Lake, black
bear waving through last summer, swaying, spored heat,
mosquitoes pilling and spouting, teeming shoulders of the bear
                         in a cleft northwest of the flat, rotting lake,
the sand colour of Pyramid Mountain lounging in the country
here, vacationing near Dillberry Lake,
the land around Chauvin, Edgerton,
along the Battle River, deep breath of it, Senlac a little
further west, shot sand roads, bird eyelid colour
of wolf willow, the pre-occupied bachelor hills there,
once you get into the country, eighty per cent sleep. The café
at Chauvin, good hamburgers, raisin pie, full of big women with
steam ploughing off them and quiet men floating in the small room.
The café at Senlac better yet, a crown of local brands along the
top of the wall (like the bar at Val Marie) and kids'
blue toys along one windowsill.
People pass through moving under the ground all the time here,
not herds of them but two or three every so often, people in their
late teens, older people from hospices in Edmonton, under the ground,
                         feathery with fishbone and carrying old water.
Water dark like the shut mountains north of Beijing, Red Snail Mountain
lifting just behind the abbot's room in the fifth century emptied
temple, its swallowed speaking bell, room with curvy, black, thick, eyebrow-
like beams and other mountains behind it with mouth-cupped shrines,
crazy bearded males-off-their-own places. Like the Dillberry Lake
area where otium sanctum flops back and forth like an eye-tipped
                         grass blade in the noses of a few animals.

TWO HILLS

In the restless intoxication of spring
when crocuses up
and grandfathers die,

sprays of flowers, brutally plastic,
lie alongside wild roses, Alberta
flowered gravesides

marking the turn of the century's
brief blaze of babies
born in rapid succession
as if, as Duras says, "in a deep, long
inhalation each year
the body of each woman took in a breath,
swelled with child,
expelled in an exhalation
a child, and then in a second inhalation
took in another"*

Stifling, hot summer winds blow the moving
and unmoving flowers, no notion of abundance

Ostriches fly from my womb to bury their awkward eyes
not realizing they have already been discovered,
followed, and recorded

The energetic rise, they are peopled by ideals.
These were blades in the wind.
This was God fearing country.

* Marguerite Duras, *The Sea Wall*

Monty Reid

THE ROAD BACK AND FORTH TO RYLEY

The mist splits open for light the way the heart
is parted for clarity. On the fields
at the edge of town white-tail browse
dark air damp on their pelage. Morning
edges down the road behind us and we've
forgotten the camera, as we always do when
deer are there, but always have it when dead skunks
and porcupines lie on the shoulders, entrails
plucked by magpies, ravens, unphotogenic crows.
Or we're late for work and can't stop.
The deer lift their heads but don't run
and the ground goes fluent with dawn.

Or the dark in mid-winter.
Through the moraine at Cooking Lake
where glaciers off the mountains and the shield
met and ground slowly into one another.
Now the snow through aspens that cover
the hummocks of till. Cones of light.
Drifts climb from the ditches, sprawl
unself-consciously over the road and we follow
the snowplow at thirty mph not
seeing anything except the blue light
diffract in white.

The girls they have for flagmen wave you down.
Euclids belly along the roadbed, the dirt
all ruts or hung in the air like an allergy
and it's summer, the girls in hardhats and
haltertops, shoulders flushed with
sun. All you can see is dust. Or farther
past the construction, where heat wraps the highway
in cellophane, the way things are packaged
so you don't see what you've got til you've paid
for it. But I could drive this road
blindfolded.

The city hoists itself into light
block by block on threads of smoke
and the traffic thickens, bumper to bumper
all the way in from Sherwood Park and when one stops
everybody does. If you were with me
you'd be nervous, stiffening every time
someone merged ahead of us, your foot
pumps an imaginary brake.
                              At night, from Ryley
the city's glare floats on the horizon like the nest
of a waterbird. In the morning, driving,
it disappears.

Anna Mioduchowska

TAWAYIK LAKE ON THE FIRST SUNDAY IN MARCH
  (*from* Elk Island National Park)

time standing still, trapped
        under layers of mortar the wind
      has ingeniously trowelled into countless waves
                going nowhere, the lake a clock face
abandoned in a blue cave

standing still, until
          two skiers step down from the shore
                slowly begin to circle: arms thrusting forward
                      in a steady rhythm, feet tunnelling through
the one in the lead

breaks trail for the second skier
        who dawdles behind, humming a different tune
                progress interrupted by frequent quarter rests
                        full stops

yet somehow

as if part of a precise mechanism
        the figures fully synchronized, along with the wind
              dogging them, within minutes it removes all trace
                    of their scent, restores the initial illusion
once again

time at a standstill, except
        for a branch jutting out of the lake's frigid depths
              where unrest lies in wait for an opportune moment
                    for the powdery spin-drift
which like the contents

of an hourglass gone mad
                whirls out of control, skinny young buffalo
                      rising from the surrounding bog

201

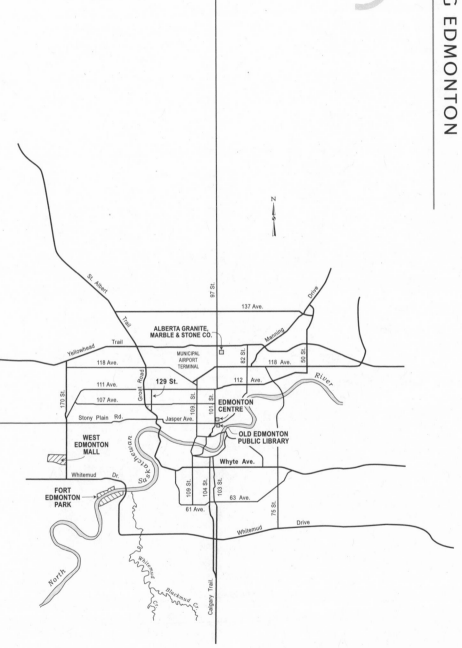

N

St. Albert

Trail

97 St.

137 Ave.

Drive

ALBERTA GRANITE,
MARBLE & STONE CO.

Manning

Yellowhead   Trail

118 Ave.

MUNICIPAL
AIRPORT
TERMINAL

82 St.

118 Ave.

50 St.

170 St.

Groat Road

111 Ave.

129 St.

109 St.

101 St.

112   Ave.

River

107 Ave.

EDMONTON
CENTRE

Stony Plain   Rd.

Jasper Ave.

OLD EDMONTON
PUBLIC LIBRARY

WEST
EDMONTON
MALL

Saskatchewan

Whyte Ave.

Whitemud   Dr.

FORT
EDMONTON
PARK

109 St.

104 St.

103 St.

63 Ave.

75 St.

61 Ave.

Whitemud   Drive

North

Whitemud

Blackmud Cr.

Cr.

Calgary Trail.

Douglas Barbour

EDMONTON OCTOBER POEM

edmonton sky: a variety
of greys, tints
of executive thought, buffaloes
without thunder growing old.

this grey parades, pervades
thought, dulls
almost the landscape.

Yet trees shine, leaves
glow yellow, orange, red
on the bluff, blow

bright onto the swaying river,

crack the cold vision
in two.

A CUP OF COFFEE IN SOLITUDE

January in Edmonton. How tenderly
the dusk comes down, a bedsheet
settled over a sick child
by a sighing mother. And the snow –
as if her bones are sifting apart
out of love, love and fear.

The planet is all silence now,
a silent turning and settling in,
as of a great shagged dog
nuzzling down to sleep.

The birds have all retreated from the siege of Moscow,
a French air dying in their throats.

Silence.

My body fills slowly with dark
as the café's plate-glass window
fills the same –

O standing grave of the world,
who fills you in?

A car passes on the muffled road.
spawning-salmon slow.

Over a field of bloodless down,
three figures leave an outdoor rink,
skates dangling darkly
from their hands,
like bagged game,
sticks propped on their shoulders
like shotguns –
a Dutch oil of an English scene.

And suddenly I know again
the supple closing of the spaniel's mouth
on the plummeted pheasant's
bloodied sheen,
the learned restraint
of the poised teeth,
the loving patience and upward look
to the coldness that kills,
the worded frost that commands.

But no one speaks
through the grass
out of the dusk.

Only a shovel on the walk
scrapes the snow, pushes back
the slab of the marble tomb.

Homeward, I will look up, again,
for a voice to command tenderness
out of the cold,
cold black.

Leonard Cohen

EDMONTON, ALBERTA,
DECEMBER 1966, 4 A.M.

Edmonton, Alberta, December 1966, 4 a.m.
When did I stop writing you?
The sandalwood is on fire in this small hotel on Jasper Street.
You've entered the room a hundred times
disguises of sari and armour and jeans,
and you sit beside me for hours
like a woman alone in a happy room.
I've sung to a thousand people
and I've written a small new song
I believe I will trust myself with the care of my soul.
I hope you have money for the winter.
I'll send you some as soon as I'm paid.
Grass and honey, the singing radiator,
the shadow of bridges on the ice
of the North Saskatchewan River,
the cold blue hospital of the sky –
it all keeps us such sweet company.

Lorne Daniel

FORT EDMONTON PARK

heat and people: we collect
on the parking lot and new boardwalks
doing our best to re-create
summer and a history as recent
as great-grandparents, lean over
cordons, peer around corners, through
chinks in relocated log houses, up
creaking staircases, reconstructing
wooden stories, constructing new
replicas in memory, building it all in
right there between last night's hockey highlights
and tonight's barbecue on the balcony

leaving on foot through dust and exhaust, drifting
from the gravel road down the riverbank
through a bluff, new poplar, we talk
fall provisions, ancestors who knew
all the wild edibles, watch
dusty bushes for rose hips
and our son, low-to-the-ground,
spots shaggy manes, snatches one without knowing
its bite; the taste strong with a history
however brief, the short white mushroom life
streaked in its own black ink

Cecelia Frey

THE OLD EDMONTON PUBLIC LIBRARY

I once had a job
in a paper dungeon
a prisoner of diaries
      maps
lives
fragile as pressed leaves
set on shelves
sorted and labelled

Each day I left my friends
               going for coffee
    their voices
        light as sun through tall windows
to begin the descent

      caught
        in a closed cage
    a hinged jaw
the elevator
         ancient and crickety
sucked me into the earth
the only way out
    to spin
words into yellow dust

I sat between paper walls
calculated cave-ins
      the possibility of survival
the stench of paper rot
filled my nostrils

Then one day I found myself
                written
legends of an old house
notes on a tribe of immigrants
entries poised
between history and dance
       one day
in my hands the words
           moved
wingless larvae
          becoming
     black moths

Gary Geddes

LAST TANGO IN EDMONTON

Was winter and the grass, aerialed,
receded into the earth, cranked by hand
or pushed down underfoot.　　No message,

its disappearance said, sullen, ingrown,
licking the first frost from the last azalea.
Was evening, a little later than usual,

that time of day when acid light
dissolves the edges of things; or rather,
perfectionist, erases the features,

all the hard-won details of hours,
till even the silhouettes themselves give up
or spread their two-dimensioned blanket

selves out on the naked earth and sleep,
dreaming their cardboard ecstasies, their pulp.
Was city, of course, slipping out of its clothes

after a good day's work: the smudged chemise,
the soiled factory apron flung across a chair,
of powdering snow.　　Beyond the ice-blue cosmetic

river the glittering tiara, tabled, winks.
And O, should I say it, punched out, expelled,
inching homeward in his shell, treacle time

spread thick upon the avenues, waiting for what
disaster, what changes of light, what jaws to strike,
to pull him downward, down into the deep, was man?

Leslie Greentree

FARGO'S, *WHYTE AVENUE*

dark ale at your hand
pale at mine
your dark head bent over a poem

three o'clock on a Thursday
I watch the solitary drinkers
the waitress
the way your hair falls over your eyes

you look up to ask
which is more phallic –
to be shot
or stabbed

you think shot
the bullet like sperm penetrating
I say stabbed
the shape of the knife
and how it enters you

we order another round
dry ribs with lemon
I watch your large hands cup the glass
bony knuckles   pared blunt nails
think of your fingers on the inside of my wrist

the sign on the chipped brick wall says
fine food and wet goods

Gerald Hill

ON LINE

Circles and right lines limit and close all bodies.
— Thomas Brown

A line down the valley of the North
Sask river over the freeze
in the hills introduces
the body of a place, its contours
and planes, the way to get through.

West on Jasper Avenue the line
picks up passengers who leave
their voices at the door and don't get on
without getting off again.

The line scores the valley top,
ends with the word *bridge* and starts
again on the other side. The river like
a line is seen to end at visible margins.

Release: the line rises up the south bank
and through Garneau's farm. Old Laurent
plows his land, his line
turns and turns.

Laurence Hutchman

RECORD COLD

Here weather is metaphor.
The Edmonton sky is high, pastel blue.
November, and I still joke with students
about this Miami of the North.
Then, nights in December
the city is a frozen inferno:
smoke blossoming into silent explosions.
Buildings glitter in a violet icy fire,
breathe reality into that paradox,
"till hell freezes over."
Here on the North Saskatchewan
I look north to nothing
and nothing moves except me.
Behind barred cells people stare;
the trees shriek like humans
as wind roars through this history of ice.
Now it is April and still we
are trapped within our cells.
Around us the snow lies
like a mad fool's crown
yet still this unbroken king
lacerates us with his sceptred words
the metaphors strike the cheeks numb.

PERSEPHONE ON 129 STREET

Winter gives up abruptly here, drops
like a penny through the torn crease
in a coat pocket. Not noticed,
as we all scamper for release
in the glinting scurry of the melting snow.

Water goes running down the street
to the languorous-but-lively beat
of Calypso tunes. *Down the way*
sways the CD in the coffeeshop,
sun shines daily on the mountain top.

At the table by the window, sits a girl
with sunlight in her hair, a ragged nest
of straw spun suddenly to gold.
Her T-shirt reads "Six Inch Nails."
She clicks the coffee mug she holds

and hums along. Outside, pedestrians
limbo into summer. A heavy man
wears his jacket open, a T-shirt
stretched across his bouncing stomach
like a beach-ball's striped skin.

Followed by a policeman, jacket
off entirely, letting the air go free.
The walkie-talkie riding at his hip
swings up and down, like the twitch
a hula dancer gives her grass skirt.

Then six young men go two by two,
like pallbearers in formation, except
it's not a coffin they have hoisted
on their denim shoulders, it's a green-
flowered sofa – a throne for the queen

of May, a chintz cortège. As they pass
one of the bearers turns to gaze
at the girl's hair shining through the glass.
She smiles and waves, and suddenly
gets up to go. She leaves the café

door open and lipstick on her cup.
It feels like summer's dancing up
from ritual darkness. All the nails
and manacles have popped loose
and we're the lucky ones who got away.

Eli Mandel

EDMONTON'S STREETS ARE NUMBERED

8400–15000
            is a street
I have no story of
            no way
this street becomes god
            or god's way
(I mean destruction's way
or a slough, the sun sunk,
. the pool a hive of eyes
            I mean
despair on the street
in the narrow way
the people shrunk
            small as a fist
            faces like fists
and muscles wound
all over their thin bones
like vines around trees
or ropes of greed
I once saw a tailor sew
for a town of friends
who put a kettle on my head)

       unstoried street
winds into (no) destruction
       (no) grief
   (no) kettle of
      fried-
   (the shrunk fish, dead
   three days lay on the murky
   sun-left sand-struck lively
   with flies shore
      deft with death

   I could not swallow)

only the snow, white explosion,
kills for my daughter
     fishful of summer
     and the unstoried houses
a fistful
      a cat sniffs
a whole summer of fish
whose skeleton lies
     a tin (awry)
         kettle

Miriam Mandel

EDMONTON, MAY 23, 1978

I must tell you
about
my walk
along
82ⁿᵈ Ave.
with
a large, tropical plant.
We were meant
for
each other.
Its leaves shaded
my fair skin
from
the burning sun
and I
placed kisses
along
the green of it –
the words we spoke
were silent
but
both understood
the endearments –
gradually
its long green
encircled my head
and
my body
and

we succeeded
finally
in startling
summer strollers
by
the passion
so clearly
surrounding us.

That plant
is
a friend
alive and well
in
Edmonton.

Erin Mouré

ALTA. GRANITE MARBLE & STONE CO. EDMONTON

i am stooped, my back
a wired crutch, immobile as
all hell; stooped & cutting
alphabet

george w harper 1875
– 1942, i am carving
your tombstone, rubber
on granite/ preparation for
sandblast –
·letters raised on black metamorphic
sparked w/ gold for
your sun, george

i stoop for you, george
my back an electric
rhythm of pain, offset
behind me, shock
transferred to your stone
george, can you feel
the current, gothic signals
stencilled thru your skull
it is 1973, george
Tuesday, or
have you forgotten this
war

my back twisted, george
listen, i stoop
for you

P.K. Page

SKYLINE

```
                            M
                E           O
        M       O   DT      N
        OO    N   MOE   T   T   M N
      DO  OENN    T   ONDOOEOEOTEMN
    EMNTNDTEDMONNEMNNDNDNODOTO N

AIRIEPRAIRIEPRAIRIEPRAIRIEPRAIRIEPRAIRIEPRAIRIEPRAIRIEPRAIRIEPR
```

ALBERTA S.P.Q.R.

Smoldering North Saskatchewan
snakes through
wooded banks
      leafless penumbras
sylvan deities
      banished by snow
      and grey towers
Arno, Brenta, Po, Tagliamento
      no Lombardy poplars
      Canadian aspens
      reach up to
      a babelled horizon

White fog
      sweat on heaven's brow
      ridges brown
      bridges rusty

Babylon from summer
Romulus has killed Remus
in downtown January.

Stephen Scobie

FEBRUARY EDMONTON

Like a love-affair dead on its feet
but refusing to admit it, winter
clings to the city.   The piles of snow
assert its long possession, and they
will not melt easily: the parting
stains them brown and dying, as if
it were blood the cars sprayed up,
splashing through puddles.   Then,
from under the snow, the scars emerge:
deep ruts in roadways, images
of what the glaciers once did;
and the hard earth brittle brown,
the grass scrubbed off its icy surface
through which plants have to break.
These scars and images claw at the spring
like a desperate lover, who leaves
stark symbols of herself behind, determined
to haunt your midsummer memory.

NOVEMBER EDMONTON

white folds
slopes down
to river
cobbled
with ice ...

ringed by
lines of light
a chimney
fatly gushes
and night
wind skimming
the slopes
tears it
to tatters ...

squat stone
shells hold
rungs of light ...

air so bright
it sings ...

Ivan Sundal

EDMONTON, 2000, SUMMER

Stone and green

Seen from the middle
of the trail bridge hung
from the LRT rib
of concrete over the river

Great croppings out
stone   up there   the towers
on the banks of the wide
lush bending
floodplains valley

And there the iron leviathan
damming the valley space
right up to the top
spilling out as waterfalls
on special occasions

The stone, the green,
the whine of River Road tires
remind me that I am from
a concrete place and time

Anne Swannell

AT THE ICE PALACE
   (*from* Mall, *a collection of poems about the West Edmonton mall*)

   1
This most public of places, this marble mall,
is really a most private one,
and into it Ed Pauperson sometimes shuffles.
He takes the bus over here from downtown
when he gets the urge – and the money –
spends the day where the snow is not,
and there's plenty happening.

Cross-legged and bony, he sits
under the green and vigorous trees,
under the sun which pours through the roof,
makes the ice glitter, the gliding figures
golden, believing that later
he might just make it to the other end
to find the thing they call Blue Thunder
or see the dolphins jump.

He knows he must keep moving
or Security'll be on his tail.
They've got a mandate to keep out vagrants
of his scent and vintage.
Ed sometimes goes through the trash cans down on Jasper,
but he knows he can't do that up here
in this cathedral of consumption,
this hall of mirrors.

2

He wishes
he had one of them wheeled jobs
they rent to scoot around in.
Then, by God, he'd get 'round some:
sail over that shiny marble
like it was water and him a schooner
with the wind behind him.

He'd find himself
some hotsy-totsy little woman called Edwina –
not one of them you see nowadays –
one of the ones he has in his mind from before.
He'd scoop flowers out of the florist's –
if he could find a florist.

Red roses. Piled in her lap.
She'd take off then,
and he'd chase her
over the marble
as far as the fountains,
where she'd throw the flowers – one at a time –
into the water shooting upwards.
The force of the fountain
would keep the blossoms jumping
and everyone would clap.

When Security came,
Ed and Edwina would rip all their clothes off
real quick like, and jump in the fountain
along with the flowers.
The trumpet of water, the sun-lit bubbles
would keep them up
rising high and forever
out of Security's reach –
clean, and sparkling, and laughing out loud.

3
He looks around, casual,
fumbles a crumpled bill from his pocket,
buys a cup of chocolate;
it tastes sweet to him, and hot enough.

John O. Thompson

STUCCO'D (EDMONTON)

Likeness makes property less lonely? No house
touches its neighbour save by resembling;
snow too blankets distinctions like a clause,
so they choose stucco, snowlike but unmelting.

If you like stanza, if you like rhyme,
shouldn't – quarrel though you might
with all its white – this module-street delight?
And stucco greys in next to no time.

James Thurgood

SMASH THE WINDOW

1

in this empty LRT station

the Métis smack pusher
calls for a country tune
– he's scary
and might be brooding
on my refusal to hold six
(whatever that meant)
so I gamble
    on the Red River Jig

he seems to read
the fluorescent glare
on the white walls
but half turns
and for the first time
    smiles

outside
moccasined feet
stir prairie dust
this tune carried on wind
past a campfire
into night lit
    by moon and stars
where eyes gleam
    from deep walls
    of dark

2
 later
on Whyte Avenue
a burly derelict with crutches
smudged jogger's sweatband
hospital bracelet
hands caked
 (I decide not to
  shake again)

when passersby don't pay
he takes on my alter ego:
cheap fuckin bastards
he calls
and in the wake
of a teenage girl:
mm – you smell beautiful

the crowd at the ice-cream logcabin
 ignores him
as he growls and barks at them
to give me money

see – soon as you get rid of one
another takes his place
says the bearded greaser
beer can in hand

play the Peace River Jig
the derelict roars

I take a chance on Big John MacNeil
like someone from the Bible
he throws down his crutches
and begins to dance

                    later
I'm playing Smash the Window
when he stops short
    bellows
that was my mother's favourite tune

    on unsteady feet
eyes burning
    turns to strangers

                    flings
    back his head and howls
to the streetlight:

that was my mother's favourite tune

Phyllis Webb

EDMONTON CENTRE, SEPT. 23/80

It was just there. It? They? Music
suddenly I come upon the
                              key cutting shop
and "Wool" and a young bassist – bronzed hair long
beyond her waist
                    Music
in the courtyard of the Centre. One can smoke
and listen to Music with little kids
lying on stomachs
                        escalator climbing with surprised
mid-day Edmontonians playing it cool
        who look askance
                        .   or turn around as the
Music mounts with them into leafy levels
of Marks and Spencers
                        staring –
The Edmonton Symphony in plain clothes fiddling
the bad vibes of Eatons and Woodwards, key shop
grinding out keys.
                    Keys!
And after the final number I'm sure I see
Maureen Forrester licking a vanilla ice-cream cone
– she waves her musical hand to a friend in the winds.
Man in cowboy hat wanders off. Chinese gentleman
moves urgently towards "Exit." Maureen takes
the escalator, strolls into Mappins.

Touchstone. She is a touchstone. Remember Maureen
the Trout Quintet that summer of '51 in Montreal?

But maybe it isn't Forrester, after all. Thirty
years later, almost, I am here
carrying nonbiodegradable plastic shopping bags
back
        to the scarey car park
                        jangling my keys

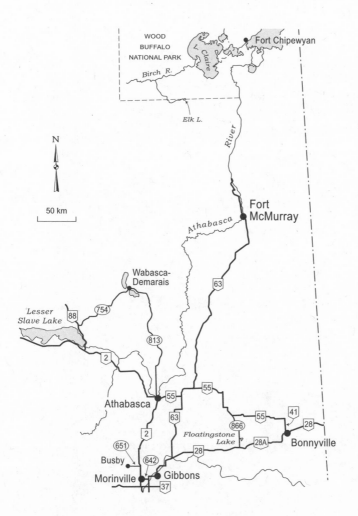

Tom Wayman

HIGHWAY 2 NORTH OF EDMONTON, ALBERTA

The glow of the city slips behind
as the car speeds into the blackness.
My high beams uncover a road
constructed during the day
across a landscape now invisible.
Out here, in the night
that is half our world,
are also trees, barns, cultivated fields.
But in light's absence
these exist unseen.

          Most of the universe
consists of darkness. The stars
and the planets huddled as near them as possible
are only an insignificant imperfection
in cold space. In this age, we bring our lamps
into the dark beyond the towns
to reveal what waits there
unaffected by our feeble spark:

     Jupiter floating among its moons,
     three hundred times more massive than the Earth,
     its outer shell immense bands of
     turbulent, swirling cloud

               or the ruined ocean liner
     that fell for hours
     into the abyss, to rest on the sea floor
     eerily upright, surrounded by a spray
     of human objects –
     cutlery, shoes, ropes, eyeglasses, stoves

as in the houses
along this highway
hidden from me, or located
by a single light
gleaming on the dark hills.

239

E.D. Blodgett

MARGINS OF MORINVILLE

tables and the treeless
pathos of cups, of calendars of months
ago, of windows welling to shallow
norths, here towns –

theirs, and whole horizons
of brides, are the pure
chance of other stars, and seas
riddled with stops

of dolphin.
        sometimes barges
sometimes green shades there are,
burdened with pears upon strands,
that break water

and windows there, windows seize
stars, and brides step
where suns fall from day
to day: but dolphins are

random to rise.   cups, perhaps,
shall have no departure.   a wind
stays for them, and slopes
of dust where doors are blank

Stephen Scobie

SONGS ON THE RADIO

here comes the night
here it comes
like a song on the radio

driving CHED, straightahead
down this suspicious highway
Streetheart's version, not
as good as Them
my mechanical judgement
remembers:

listening with Leisha
in front of the fire, the only
time I ever visited
her home in Irvine; her father
asleep in his chair oblivious
to her mad German mother
screaming: and nothing else
remains in my mind: the image
so vague I can't even be sure
I didn't invent it

except for the song: Van Morrison
sang it, with Them
from Northern Ireland, a raw
unfinished country, breaking
apart: a raw
unfinished emotion, night
the long the long the lonely night

and Leisha, whom I never
decided to be in love with, she
and I knew what it meant
sometimes in the dark
old streets of our city, our cold
and ancient city:
cold in her bones, she wrote me
once I had gone, once at a distance
of five thousand miles
I could admit I loved her
far too late
for any good it might have done, here
comes the night
the night the night the lonely night

playing now on my radio
a botched-up version
somewhere near Gibbons, Alberta
on Highway 37, heading north
with a fine snow falling
into my eyes

E.D. Blodgett

RETURNING TO BUSBY, ALTA.

After we put the rest of Georges Bugnet
to ground, walking apart beneath the blue
and static sky, I found myself along
the road to Busby, white going away
past the lake and old, arthritic trees,
beyond the coyote staring in the field

of white at me along the road against
the fence – myself, my eyes open, complete
with solitudes untouched by wind, the clear
distance of solitude, a shack before
it leans in time, the scentless air, a **then**
of no forgetting, pristine solitudes

of winter 1905 taking stands
within my eyes. Wherever I saw you old,
enclosed in rooms that age sits through,
wherever you were, immobile, panes of snow
hedged us inside, the yard through the window set
wherever now would be. Perhaps that is all

the **now** there is – angles of white roof,
ends of old grass against a wall,
flawless shadow waiting for time to come,
a time for coyotes, watching, uncertain yet
where to move. Do coyotes sit with us,
unseen, edging the margins of 1905,

coyotes entering glass, the walls of light
between us and now? It is enough to ask
questions of fences, speaking of coyotes so,
walking into Busby, the store closed,
clouds suspended in glass, a long cry
in the air and silence as grass bent to ground.

WRITING NORTHEASTERN ALBERTA & THE BOREAL FORESTS

Robert Boates

LATE SEPTEMBER

Driving north to Athabasca
through seasons fighting
for conquest of an afternoon.
A crack across the windshield
suggests lightning; a bolt
sealed in a paperweight
like a scorpion, its tail
poised to strike.

The day is full of potential slaughter.
Sleet-covered cattle and buffalo
wait to be bred for market.
Deer evade searching eyes.
Our eyes. Smaller
animals remain concealed
for death wears wings
and is owl-swift.

We are small beneath this sky,
travelling toward the horizon.
That rainbow in the distance,
a scythe, a promise.

Richard Hornsey

TESTING THE SPRING RUN

Up in Wabasca
the Metis swerve abandoned
through a relic world
of crumpled cars and tarpaper.
The creek banks are slippery
slaughterhouse floors
cluttered with torn pike heads
and curled mother-of-pearl
pickerel skins.

We are too late.
Muddy, limb-tangled veins,
the brimming cuts flow slowly.

We have passed much here.
The two trucks welded together
by an impact so fierce
that both windshields were gone
and the steering columns had wilted.
The station attendant who told us
that Sunday was a dangerous day.
Drunks careening forty miles home
over the rolling gravel.

On one of the turns we saw a Pontiac
hood-deep in ditch water.
The survivors were walking toward us
clear-eyed and determined.
Going some place.

It was raining.
We hadn't caught a thing.
We drove on.

73L   23   2   79

forgiveness
is an appearance
that floats

on a semblance
of water

Floatingstone Lake
this rock
torn

of its formation
set by ice
here

called an erratic
but the error
as always

is human
the Crees called
it assinkagana

the stone
that floats

and we
as we do
all history

repeat
this ignorance

and this
grace

Stephen Scobie

ON THE ROAD TO BONNYVILLE

On the road, the snow is dancing
in time to the music, in small
white whirlwinds before me:

      behind there is nothing
      to be seen in the mirror
      white

of the snow that gathers behind us
pulled like a parachute into
the speed of our passing: in front

when a truck overtakes
we are driving snowblind
into a memory.

      Meanwhile we talk about poets
      especially
      the ones we don't like

and Doug takes out his cassettes
balancing the music on his knees
as he flays some phony surrealist:

      the collected reviews
      of Linda Ronstadt
      in time to the music: well,

I guess it doesn't matter any more.

Colleen Thibaudeau

ALL MY NEPHEWS HAVE GONE TO THE TAR SANDS

All my nephews have gone to the Tar Sands.
I find it difficult to write to them.
One slept in his truck all winter
40 below and no postal code.
One helpless watched his little farm-girl wife
Let the home-sick tears freeze into terrible silence.
One fathered what I nickname
The Tar Sands Baby. I'm wondering,
Nephews, is what I feel writing you neon letters
The same feeling that maybe my grandma had
When she would turn and look out the window,
(Staring just above the frostline & geraniums)
Her voice flat & inevitable: "They've gone to the West."
All my nephews have gone to the Tar Sands.
I find it difficult to write to them.

Eva Tihanyi

ELK LAKE IMPERATIVE

Think north

Think of blueberries in August,
the silver arrowpaths of starlight
piercing the rich red orchards
of the blood's harvest

Think of spruce, poplar, pine –
an incantation of trees
among the night-drenched rocks,
the wizardry of moonlight
on ebony green water

And remember the morning,
your bones
shifting comfortably in sunlight,
your face hot with a blush
of autumnal cold

This is the earth's secret,
the untamed song of body,
the cherished fuel
we hoard for winter

Tim Bowling

FINAL NIGHT IN FORT CHIPEWYAN

On frozen Athabasca Lake
I stood alone, several hundred strides
from shore. February. Twilight. Somewhere
my name was written down in books, in files,
on old letters, called up on screens. Somewhere
a woman spoke my name to a friend, and smiled.
What happens when even the dogs fall silent
north of everything you've ever known?
Suddenly, it was as though the universe
had slipped beneath the ice, and my heart
sent a faint signal to my life on earth.
If someone had called my name just then,
I would not have turned. I was a new language
given substance by the kindness of the wind.
The moon rose slowly, detached from the snow.
I returned to my long sentence and my story,
found the low stars of the town, and headed in.

11

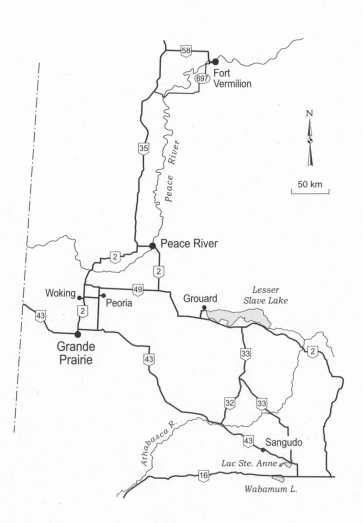

Eli Mandel

WABAMUN

1
lake
    holds
            sun moon stars

            trees
                    hold

stars moon sun

2
thunder
        and sky
towel
        wet sand
in yellow light

            yesterday

3
on water
many suns
            here there
fires then
silent comedians
gulls
perch jumping

4
only
    waves   motion
    sun   dancing

no   sun

only
    light
hurting
in its
    endless
dance

5
each day I
step
    farther
into dark water

once I will
know
    no longer

whether
    that one
floating
    is myself
or the light
    one
standing
    on the red
pier

6
moon train on causeway

coal cars

      a white moon

7
to have come to this
simplicity
      to know
only
    the absolute
calm
   lake

   before

   night

8
clover   smell
sweet stars in a green sky

white sweet stars
blossom in a green sky

clover   stars
in a white sky

white
   stars

Michael Henry

PILGRIMAGE TO LAC STE. ANNE

At her patron's feast
the pristine white of Lac Ste. Anne
blistered in the heat.

Metis pilgrims trail
along dusty potholed roads
fully-clothed they wade into the lake
cupping hands to drink the water.

it rains as if on cue –
the mission shrine varnished fresh again.

a priest leads out the Procession of the Cross –
chanting kneeling praying
a stream of pilgrims
flows past the stations of the Cross
flows to the grotto
where like spray the crowds disperse
their faith replenished
by the miracle of rain.

mission shrine and chapel
now boarded up another year.

'St. Theresa patron of the mission pray for us.'

Jan Zwicky

PASSING SANGUDO

Sangudo, of the long hill and
the river flats; of the long shadows
in the river valley; Sangudo,
of the early evening, in the summertime,
on the way out Highway 43 after
a day in the city: how ugly
I used to think your name; and how,
unhappy in the car, unhappy
at the prospect of unwelcome dressed as welcome
that awaited us, I believed,
as we all believe, that growing up
meant never having to come back;
how, much though I deplored our town,
I was glad it wasn't you: that much smaller,
that much shabbier, the mud a little deeper,
the store fronts just that much more stark.
It must have rained most days that we drove past
because it rained most days then – or so it seems;
but of course plenty of times it must
have been winter, it being winter most of the year then
– or so it seems. And indeed the one recurring
nightmare of childhood, tobaganning down the river bank
and falling through the ice, with my father for some reason,
as well as my sister, and all of us drowning, silently, the ice
growing rigid over us in jagged chunks – that winter dream
was set outside Sangudo, just where the highway
crosses the Pembina, twenty feet
downstream from the bridge.
So it is mildly surprising – like discovering, at 40,
your handwriting closely resembles your great-uncle's
though you've never met – surprising I should find
that what I remember now
is neither rain nor snow, but long shadows,

early summer twilight, the sweet forgiving
roll of the land, the car's movement through it
steady, a quiet humming, exactly as it should be,
coming from nowhere, destined nowhere, simply moving,
driving past Sangudo, over the dark brown Pembina,
up the long hill, home.

Rajinderpal Pal

SOLSTICE

summer solstice on lesser slave lake
the midnight sun
a dim glow on the horizon
we watched long enough to turn to sunrise

you leaned against me
and your body numbed the places where we touched
insides of thighs
a shoulder

we awoke to the sound of swimmers
slapping water
and a grey morning rain
circles within circles
on the lake's dark surface

Greg Simison

GROUARD CEMETERY

over the years
the elements have done their job well ...
you can barely read the collapsing wooden crosses now
but we know who lie here,
four generations of metis and indian
two dozen priests and nuns
and in the poorer suburbs
at the foot of the slope
tight against the picket fence
homesick remittance men
unclaimed victims of Klondike fever
lost to bar brawls and blizzards
a few worn-out farmers
free at last from the blackflies and futility

and me
sprawled against a grassy mound
recording faded names and dates
random thoughts
delving for bonanza-sized nuggets
hoping to crop some sort of sense
from this tight-fisted wilderness

Erin Mouré

GRANDE PRAIRIE: SO FAR FROM POLAND

Gone to my grandmother's house in the gully,
white light of summer shocked the air into bright being,
all I remember is green
& my grandmother standing out in the shade of huge cabbages,
open as mouths,
manure packed smelly around the roots,
gurgle of wet creek behind.
I followed wild rows of the yard to find her,
she talked the guttural words I did not know & lifted my small bones
over the cabbages, against
her wide apron of flowers.

From her arms I could see the gully, & my brothers arriving,
running along in their shorts & toy pistols,
the ground solid & green everywhere, hot-smelling,
the air steaming
white
What she would tell me, & I couldn't answer, just shied away
stupid & went back to the toy pistols,
the shouts of my brothers,
running faster than the heat in the garden
to keep cool,
as she stood & watched us, worried about creek-banks
& the mad growing cabbages,
locked forever in her language that she brought so far from Poland,
stockpiled like a garden, where she stayed
& did not grow out of

Tom Howe

PROSSER'S HOUSE

Driving somewhere between two Alberta Wheat Pool towns
named Peoria and Woking
in the Peace River country
     squared land
       where old farm shacks with weather-grey boards
       begin to loosen toward the earth
       and a man can point to the home he was born in
       across his own field
we were looking for the Woking road and weren't expecting
to see a sign

at lunch-time we came across an abandoned farm house
slowly giving itself back to the ground
due only to a sudden neglect   triggering the process
as though one day its tenants
rushed out to the corner for a moment
and never returned
       the driveway had disappeared
       the outhouse was leaning
       and siding just beginning to fall off
an old house no longer indicating occupancy
except by the chipmunks who had moved in

I found a sunken faded armchair for furniture inside
and the room scheme still intact
the stairs to the bedrooms held my weight
and only creaked a little although the ceiling above me
had fallen out
the bedrooms were empty and nothing would say
that a couple had held each other close
while tiny animals scurried outside

I found medicaments in the kitchen
 Backrite tablets for kidney ailments
 Na Dru Co fly repulser paste
 Vitamin B capsules
 and a few old empty bottles
 one bore a Grande Prairie prescription label
 advising Gladys and Trella Prosser to gargle
 twice daily when necessary

and nothing else that you could say was ever owned by someone
nothing but the house itself
the planks and boards that Prosser nailed together in a
 homesteading
 dream made real by wood and design
 enlivened by personal habits like Trella gargling
 and Gladys frying bacon a dog slurped water in the corner
 Prosser's women bustled in cotton dresses
 at night lay warm in beds that are gone
 through all the windy winter nights until the day
 Prosser whispered "enough" at his dream
 and was gone
hard to say what happened
the house is quiet and says nothing more
so quiet in the long afternoon
that only the faint sound of Prosser
nailing his last shingle
sounds at all in the tiny dancing leaves
and only for the chipmunks

James Wreford Watson

THE NORTHLANDS, PEACE RIVER: ALTA.

(1)
The valley
a sheer
      incandescence
            all at once
of fall aspen
      turned pure gold
        glows
with a furnaced beauty:
nothing but
the bitter north
could hold such a fierceness out
      of such a wonder
it's as if this hour
was meant to stop the mouth
of all time's grief

cry if we must
          not the fear
of the long winter waiting us
but this short marvel which
        has in it all
    all
     loveliness.

(2)
Mad with butterflies
                    the flower-starred field
of this high-north alfalfa land
makes of the fall of time
all at once
                    time's stand!
What day's more
                    – but I mean –
                                        crazed
with the sheer happiness
                    of being alive
than this storm of winged wonder
                                        loosed
in the bloom-rich plain?
For this
                spring burst the iron-hard ground
                    with its tender green,
the seethed-with-summer air
                                        for this
made sap run nectar;
                        let
the wine of the year's joy
                            in us, too
a wing-drunk prairie get.

(3)
Look how
in the long low northern light
evening calls out the land,

        houses wink eyes
        walls leap to view
    hills
are tricked in sheer silk:

        there is
a living glow along the valley's rim
even the gullies shine,

        wind in the hay
is like a play of colts,

        sloughs shimmer like
quick dragonflies,

        clouds go by
belly-side blown,

        trees too seem all underskirts
        swung in a golden breeze
men scissor their shadows in huge lit strides
women are haloed in flame in the last rays.

Pity the South with its shut-down eves,
here summer goes into the midnight hours
the low and slanting light

        fingers the land
        with lingering care.
Where else will you find the like
    where
are the fields so pearled
the valley side beaten from silver

           so?
However doomed, by what return of winter,
    here
is an hour not matched in pride.

Aleksei Kazuk

WALKING INTO THE MANDALA: FORT VERMILLION

His long feet grip the vibration, hips and spine
Again riding the waves; vulnerable as the eyes of apes,
He is taunted by the heavens, risen and still.

Memories of a girl in Gibraltar lovely have hardened;
An obsidian prow, cleaving breakers, he escapes wrath of passion
With intrigue of oil and radar.

Three sections of dirt near Fort Vermillion Alberta is vast,
Yet the hardened fire of black rocks squint with the farmer,
From the pitching land, at the sun.

Memories of the ruined Ukraine, Toronto, the Dust Bowl,
Bulldozed onto smoking convoys of cleared poplar,
That grid the sky, help grid the land.

Bulk of the wife filling cotton print, she steadies the ploughing;
Rides her potato garden implacable under smudge-fire,
Committed to the man.

Vancouver towers are striped with clouds thick as kelp.
In Nunavit, Mounties interrogate the lack of fences.
In Ottawa, fools torch their eyes with dollars.

His *"Ya!"* wide under square brows, not a round thing in sight,
Taras' stride is firm, walking into the mandala of his field,
Little shocks creeping around his boots.

The roads are pungent with tinge of towns burned to the ground
On another steppe, and the stench of immigrant ships.
The sun locks her milk up under the Arctic Plate, as before.

The tenant above rearranges furniture on Sundays; my basement
Room cluttered with books and drafts of poems like this one.
Winds lust lonely on the Horn Plateau.

Miriam Waddington

WAITING IN ALBERTA

I am sitting in
a very remote
vast faraway
corner of Alberta,
the fourth corner
to be exact   and
although it is
June the snow is
flying but I know
it is only summer
snow and will be
over in an hour
so I make myself
comfortable   fold
a triangle of
lawn over my lap
a few foothills
over my shoulders
put on my bifocals
plug in the heating
pad and though I
know it will even-
tually kill me
I light a cigar-
ette and I watch
the first buildings
go up   then all
the lights go on
they look like
frozen grapes in
the garden of Eden
or like glass fruits

hung on tall motion-
less trees but the
air is clear as
water   not like in
Toronto;

And I think from
my very remote
corner of Alberta
that after all this
is a pretty clever
miraculous world
where I can sit
small as anything
in such a big corner
of it and the only
archaic creatures
are us people   every-
thing else is so
up-to-date   buildings
plug-ins   programming
for everything except
us people who can
still even make
love in the old
style if we feel
like it   but I like
just sitting here
with the lawn on
my lap waiting for
the sun to come
out so the orange

prairie poppies
can unwilt and
hold their heads
up again   and the
winds can go to
sleep   and I can
get on with my work.

ADAM, IAN: "The Big Rocks" in *Blue Buffalo*, 1, 2 (Spring 1983). "In Calgary These Things" in *Encounter*. Ladysmith, Quebec: Ladysmith Press, 1973. "Job Description" in *The Prairie Journal of Canadian Literature*, 18 (1992). "Trip to Banff" in *Songs from the Star Motel*. Red Deer: Red Deer College Press, 1983.

ARMSTRONG, TAMMY: "Columbia Ice Field" from *Bogman's Music*. Vancouver: Anvil Press, 2001. Used with permission of the publisher.

AVISON, MARGARET: "Banff" from "Always Now" (*The Collected Poems*, vol. 1) published by The Porcupine's Quill (Toronto), 2003.

BARBOUR, DOUGLAS: "Edmonton October Poem" in *Twelve Prairie Poets*, Laurence Ricou, ed. Ottawa: Oberon Press, 1976. "in Maligne Canyon" in *Shore Lines*. Winnipeg: Turnstone Press, 1979.

BARTON, JOHN: "This Side of the Border" in *Canadian Literature*, 144 (Spring 1995).

BEARDSLEY, DOUG: "Jasper Bears" in *Inside Passage*. Saskatoon: Thistledown Press, 1993.

BISHOP, BONNIE: "The Rumsey Moraine" in *Elaborate Beasts*. Red Deer: Red Deer College Press, 1988.

BLODGETT, E.D.: "Returning to Busby, Alta." in *Arché/Elegies*. Edmonton: Longspoon Press, 1983. "margins of Morinville" in *Take Away the Names*. Toronto: Coach House Press, 1975.

BOATES, ROBERT: "Late September" in *The Good Life*. Hamilton: Cactus Tree Press, 1990.

BOWERING, GEORGE: "calgary," "high river alberta" & "it's the climate" in *Rocky Mountain Foot*. Toronto: McClelland and Stewart, 1968.

BOWLING, TIM: "A Cup of Coffee in Solitude" & "Midday, Midsummer" in *Darkness and Silence*. Roberts Creek, B.C.: Nightwood Editions, 2001. "Cemetery at Olds" & "Final Night in Fort Chipewyan" in *The Thin Smoke of the Heart*. Montreal and Kingston: McGill-Queen's University Press, 2000.

BOYDOL, JAN: "Color Hillcrest Dead" in *Absinthe*, 6, 2 (December 1993).

BURLES, GORDON: "Reunion" in *contemporary verse two*, 7, 2 (April 1983).

BURNETT, MURDOCH: "Boys or the River" in *The Long Distance and Other Poems 1981-1986*. Cochrane, Alberta: Westlands, 1987.

CAMPBELL, ANNE: "Calgary City Wind" in *Dandelion*, 6 (1979). By Anne Campbell, Regina.

CHAN, WEYMAN: "Written on Water" in *Before a Blue Sky Moon*. Calgary: Frontenac House, 2002.

COHEN, LEONARD: "Edmonton, Alberta, December 1966, 4 a.m." in *Selected Poems, 1956–1968*. Toronto: McClelland & Stewart, 1968.

COOLEY, DENNIS: "labiarinth" from *Dedications*. Winnipeg: Turnstone Press, 1988. "labiarinth" was originally published by Thistledown Press.

CRATE, JOAN: "Gleichen" in *Native Poetry in Canada: A Contemporary Anthology*, Jeanette C. Armstrong and Lally Grauer, eds.. Peterborough: Broadview Press, 2001.

CULLEN, MICHAEL: "wind down waterton" in *NeWest Review*, 3, 10 (June 1978).

DABYDEEN, CYRIL: "By Lake Minnewanka" in *Six Ottawa Poets*. Oakville: Mosaic Press, 1990.

DANIEL, LORNE: "Fort Edmonton Park," "Season of Leaving" & "Winter at the Banff School" in *Towards a New Compass*. Saskatoon: Thistledown Press, 1978.

DEWIEL, ALEXA: "Two Hills" in *Dandelion*, 13, 2 (Fall/Winter 1986).

DEWINETZ, JASON: "Badlands" in *Moving to the Clear*. Edmonton: NeWest Press, 2002. Reprinted with permission of NeWest Publishers.

FITZPATRICK, RYAN: "From the Ogden Shops" in *fillingStation*, 22 (2001).

FREY, CECELIA: "The Old Edmonton Public Library" & "Woman in a potato field north of Nanton" in *Songs Like White Apples Tasted*. Calgary: Bayeux Arts, 1998. "Under the Louise Bridge" in *Contemporary Voice Two*, 13, 1 (Spring 1990). "Wind at Oyen, alta." in *The Least You Can Do Is Sing*. Edmonton: Longspoon Press, 1982.

GEDDES, GARY: "Last Tango in Edmonton" in *Changes of State*. Moose Jaw: Coteau Books, 1986.

GHAI, GAIL: "On a Winter Hill Overlooking Calgary" in *Glass Canyons: A Collection of Calgary Fiction and Poetry*, Ian Adam, ed. Edmonton: NeWest Press, 1985. My thanks to the editors of *Glass Canyons* in which the poem first appeared – Gail Ghai.

GODIN, DEBORAH: "Time / Lapse Calgary as Bremen" in *Troubling a Star*. Waterloo: Penumbra Press, 1989.

GREEN, JIM: "Power Line to Sunshine" in *Beyond Here*. Saskatoon: Thistledown Press, 1983.

GREENTREE, LESLIE: "Fargo's, Whyte Avenue" in *go-go dancing*. Calgary: Frontenac House, 2003.

HANSEN, VIVIAN: "Wolf Willow against the bridge" in *The Prairie Journal of Canadian Literature*, 33 (1999).

HENIHAN, TOM: "Bow Valley" in *A Further Exile*. Victoria: Ekstasis Editions, 2002.

HENRY, MICHAEL: "Pilgrimage to Lac Ste. Anne" in *Contemporary Verse II*, 4, 4 (Spring 1980).

HILDEBRANDT, WALTER: "Brooks Aqueduct" in *Brooks Coming Home*. Calgary: Bayeux Arts, 1996.

HILL, GERALD: "Sisters of the Garden" in *Paperwork: Contemporary Poems from the Job*, Tom Wayman, ed. Madiera Park, B.C.: Harbour Publishing, 1991. "On Line" in *NeWest Review*, 13, 9 (May 1988).

HILLES, ROBERT: "Progress" reprinted from *Finding the Lights On*. Toronto: Wolsak and Wynn Publishers Ltd., 1991. "When Light Transforms Flesh" in *Outlasting the Landscape*. Saskatoon: Thistledown Press, 1989.

HOLMES, NANCY: "Calgary Mirage" in *Valancy and the New World*. Vernon B.C.: Kalamalka New Writers Society, 1988. "The Right Frame of Mind" in *The Road Home: New Stories from Alberta Writers*, Fred Stenson, ed. Edmonton: Reidmore Books, 1992 (now called "Wrong Frame of Mind" in *Adultery Poems*, published by Ronsdale Press).

HORNSEY, RICHARD: "The Rocky Mountain Summer Movie" & "Testing the Spring Run" in *Where Roads and Rivers Lead*. Fredericton: Fiddlehead Poetry Books, 1979.

HOWE, TOM: "Prosser's House" in *Poems of a Snow-Eyed Country,* Richard Woollatt and Raymond Souster, eds. Don Mills, Ontario: Academic Press Canada, 1980.

HUNTER, AISLINN: "Frank Slide, Alberta" in *Into the Early Hours.* Vancouver: Raincoast Books, 2001. Reprinted by permission of Polestar Books.

HUNTER, BRUCE: "For My Brother Daniel" & "Wishbone" in *Benchmark*. Saskatoon: Thistledown Press, 1982. "Meditations on the Improbable History of a Small Town" in *Coming Home from Home.* Saskatoon: Thistledown Press, 2000. "Slow Learner" in *In the Clear: A Contemporary Canadian Poetry Anthology,* Allan Forrie, et al, eds. Toronto: Thistledown Press, 1998.

HUTCHMAN, LAURENCE: "Record Cold" in *Contemporary Verse II*, 7, 2 (April 1983).

ITO, SALLY: "At the Reynolds Museum, Wetaskiwin, Alberta" in *Season of Mercy.* Roberts Creek, B.C.: Nightwood Editions, 1999.

JOHNSON, PAULINE: "Calgary of the Plains" in *Flint and Feather: The Complete Poems.* Toronto: Hodder & Stoughton, 1972.

KAZUK, ALEKSEI: "Walking Into the Mandala: Fort Vermillion" in *The Prairie Journal of Canadian Literature*, 32 (1999).

KROETSCH, ROBERT: "Horsetail sonnet" copyright 1986, Robert Kroetsch. From *Dandelion,* 1986. "Seed Catalogue" copyright 1989, Robert Kroetsch. From *Completed Field Notes: The Long Poems* (originally published by McClelland and Stewart, now available from University of Alberta Press).

LAM, FIONA: "Departure (Highway to Lake Louise)" in *New Quarterly*, 31, 4 (Winter 2001).

LATTA, WILLIAM: "Heat Near Banff" in *Summer's Bright Blood*. Saskatoon: Thistledown Press, 1976.

LILBURN, TIM: "Hearing," "Kill-site" & "Now, Lifted, Now" in *Kill-site.* Toronto: McClelland and Stewart, 2003.

MAJOR, ALICE: "Near Red Deer" & "South of Stettler" in *Lattice of the Years*. Calgary: Bayeux Arts, 1998. "Persephone on 129 Street" in *Tales for an Urban Sky*. Fredericton: Broken Jaw Press, 1999.

MALTMAN, KIM: "Ice Fishing Cessford Lake" in *Branch Lines*. Saskatoon: Thistledown Press, 1982. "Yamnuska" in *The Country of Mapmakers*. Fredericton: Fiddlehead Books, 1977.

MANDEL, ELI: "Edmonton's Streets Are Numbered" & "Wabamun" in *The Other Harmony: The Collected Poems of Eli Mandel*. Regina: Canadian Plains Research Centre, 2000.

MANDEL, MIRIAM: "Edmonton, May 23, 1978" in *The Collected Poems of Miriam Mandel*. Edmonton: Longspoon Press and NeWest Press, 1984.

MARTY, SID: "Death Song for the Oldman" in *The Road Home: New Stories from Alberta Writers,* Fred Stenson, ed. Edmonton: Reidmore Books, 1992. "Medicine Hat" in *Twelve Prairie Poets*, Laurence Ricou, ed. Ottawa: Oberon Press, 1976. "The Sand Pile" in *ARC*, 1 (Spring 1978). "Saskatchewan Crossing Café" in *Headwaters*. Toronto: McClelland and Stewart, 1973. "Yellowhead" in *Headwaters*. Toronto: McClelland and Stewart, 1993.

MCFADDEN, DAVID: "Mountain Air" in *On the Road Again*. Toronto: McClelland and Stewart, 1978.

MCKINNON, BARRY: "untitled" in *The Alberta Diamond Jubilee Anthology*, John W. Chalmers, ed. Edmonton: Hurtig, 1979.

MICHIE, ERIN: "The Willows at Weaselhead" in *Grain*, 29, 1 (Summer 2001).

MILLER, DEBORAH: "Pictures from the Stampede" in *I Will Burn Candles*. Calgary: Bayeux Arts, 1995.

MIODUCHOWSKA, ANNA: "Tawayik Lake on the First Sunday in March" in *Other Voices*, 11, 1 (Spring 1996).

MOIR, JAMES M.: "This City by the Bow" in *Glass Canyons: A Collection of Calgary Fiction and Poetry*, Ian Adam, ed. Edmonton: NeWest Press, 1985.

MORTON, COLIN: "at bankhead" in *Dandelion*, 7, 1 (1980). "Calgary '80" in *In Transit*. Saskatoon: Thistledown Press, 1981.

MOURÉ, ERIN: "alta, granite marble & stone co. edmonton" in *Empire, York Street*. Toronto: Anansi, 1979. "Cardiac Grizzlies," "Grande Prairie: So Far From Poland" & "Westerose" from *Wanted Alive (c.1983)* by Erin Mouré. Reprinted with permission of House of Anansi Press. "South-West, or Altadore" and "Seebe" by Erin Mouré appeared in *WSW (West South West)* published by Vehicule Press (1989).

NOBLE, CHARLES: "Banff: Space / Time Swindle" in *Haywire Rainbow*. Erin, Ontario: Press Porcepic, 1978. "Mnemonic Without Portfolio" in *Afternoon Starlight*. Saskatoon: Thistledown Press, 1982. "Props64" in *Let's Hear It For Them*. Winnipeg: Thistledown Press, 1990.

PAGE, P.K.: "Skyline" in *The Hidden Room: Collected Poems*. Erin, Ontario: The Porcupine's Quill, 1997. "Skyline" from the "Hidden Room" (in two volumes) by P.K. Page, published by the Porcupine's Quill (Erin, Ontario), 1997.

PAL, RAJINDERPAL: "solstice" & "trust" in *pulse*. Vancouver: Arsenal Pulp Press, 2002.

PIERSON, RUTH ROACH: "Up Tunnel Mountain Trail" in *Vantage 2000: Poems from the National Poetry Contest and Canadian Youth Poetry Competition*. Vancouver: Ronsdale Press (League of Canadian Poets), 2000.

PIVATO, JOSEPH: "Edmonton S.P.Q.R." in *Roman Candles: An Anthology of Poems by Seventeen Italo-Canadian Poets*, Pier Giorgio di Cicco, ed. Oakville: Mosaic Press, 1984.

REES, ROBERTA: "Because Calgary" in *Eyes Like Progress*. London, Ontario: Brick Books, 1992.

REID, D.C.: "Drying Out Again" in *Dandelion*, 13, 1 (Spring/Summer 1986).

REID, MONTY: "73L 23 2 79" in *The Alternative Guide*. Red Deer: Red Deer College Press, 1998. "Bonebed: Dinosaur Provincial Park" in *NeWest Review*, 16, 6 (August/September 1991). "The Alumni Game at Lacombe Arena" & "The Road Back and Forth to Ryley" in *The Life of Ryley*. Saskatoon: Thistledown Press, 1981. "Writing-on-Stone" in *Dog Sleeps: Irritated Texts*. Edmonton: NeWest Publishers, 1993.

RICKEY, R.: "this way crowsnest" in *absinthe*, 6, 2 (December 1993).

RIVARD, KEN: "Gull Lake Alphabet" & "Turner Valley" in *Kiss Me Down to Size*. Saskatoon: Thistledown Press, 1983.

SCOBIE, STEPHEN: "February Edmonton" in *The Rooms We Are: Poems 1970–1971*. Victoria: The Sono Nis Press, 1974. "On the Road to Bonnyville" & "Songs on the Radio" in *A Grand Memory for Forgetting*. Edmonton: Longspoon Press, 1981. "Songs on the radio" also included in *The Spaces In Between: Selected Poems, 1965-2001*, Edmonton: NeWest Press, 2003.

SERAFINO, ALLAN: "Hay Rolls Near Millarville" in *Tilted to the Plane of the World: Short Stories and Poetry, A Calgary Collection,* Judy Galbraith, ed. Calgary: Galbraith Publishing, 1987.

SHILLINGTON, JOAN: "I Was Born Alberta" in *FreeFall,* 11, 2 (Fall 2001).

SIMISON, GREG: "Grouard Cemetery" in ARC, 8–9 (Spring-Summer 1983).

SOKOLOFF, CAROL ANN: "Great Divide" in *Eternal Lake O'Hara.* Victoria: Ekstasis Editions, 1993.

SOLIE, KAREN: "Java Shop, Fort Macleod" & "Suffield" in *Short Haul Engine.* London, Ontario: Brick Books, 2001.

STAMP, ROBERT: "A City Built for Speed" in *The Prairie Journal of Canadian Literature,* 38 (2002). "Energy to Burn" in *Alberta Views,* November/December 2001.

STEPHANSSON, STEPHAN: "My Region" in *Selected Prose & Poetry.* Translated by Kristjana Gunnars. Red Deer: Red Deer College Press, 1988.

STEVENS, PETER: "November Edmonton" in *A Few Myths.* Vancouver: Talonbooks, 1971.

SUNDAL, IVAN: "Edmonton, 2000, Summer" in *Stroll of Poets: 2000 Anthology.* Edmonton: 2000.

SWANNELL, ANNE: "At the Ice Palace" in *Canadian Literature,* 129 (Summer 1991).

TESSIER, VANNA: "Stone Jack" in *The Prairie Journal of Canadian Literature,* 38 (2002).

THIBAUDEAU, COLLEEN: "All My Nephews Have Gone to the Tar Sands" in *The Maple Laugh Forever: An Anthology of Comic Canadian Poetry,* Douglas Barbour and Stephen Scobie, eds.. Edmonton: Hurtig, 1981.

THOMPSON, JOHN O.: "Coal Lake" in *The Gates of Even.* Victoria: Ekstasis Editions, 2002. "Fuel Crisis" & "Stucco'd (Edmonton)" in *Echo and Montana.* Edmonton: Longspoon Press, 1980.

THURGOOD, JAMES: "smash the window" in *Fiddlehead,* 184 (Summer 1995).

TIHANYI, EVA: "Elk Lake Imperative" in *In the Clear: A Contemporary Canadian Poetry Anthology,* Allan Forrie, et al, eds. Saskatoon: Thistledown Press, 1998.

TRAINER, YVONNE: "1912" in *Tom Three Persons.* Calgary: Frontenac House, 2002. "What can Anybody See?" in *Everything Happens At Once.* Fredericton: Fiddlehead Poetry Books, 1986.

VAN HERK, ARITHA: "Quadrant Four: Outskirts of outskirts" from *a/long prairie lines,* edited by Daniel Lenoski, Winnipeg: Turnstone Press, 1989. Reprinted with permission of Turnstone Press.

VAN STELTEN, ROSALEE: "Didsbury Auction" & "The Three Sisters" in *Pattern of Genes.* Calgary: Frontenac House, 2001. "Didsbury Auction" copyright 1997, 2001, Rosalee Van Stelten. Used with permission. "The Three Sisters" copyright 2002, Rosalee van Stelten. Used with permission.

WADDINGTON, MIRIAM: "Mountain Interval 11" in *The Last Landscape.* Toronto: Oxford University Press, 1992. "Waiting in Alberta" in *Collected Poems.* Toronto: Oxford University Press, 1986.

WATSON, JAMES WREFORD: "The Northlands, Peace River: Alta." in *Countryside Canada.* Fredericton: Fiddlehead Poetry Books, 1979.

WATSON, WILFRED: "In the Cemetery of the Sun" in *Friday's Child.* London: Faber and Faber, 1955.

WAYMAN, TOM: "A Reason" in *The Face of John Munro*. Madeira Park, B.C.: Harbour Publishing, 1986. "Highway 2 North of Edmonton, Alberta" in *In a Small House on the Outskirts of Heaven*. Madeira Park, B.C.: Harbour Publishing, 1989.

WEBB, PHYLLIS: "Edmonton Centre, Sept. 23/80" in *The Maple Laugh Forever: An Anthology of Comic Canadian Poetry,* Douglas Barbour and Stephen Scobie, eds. Edmonton: Hurtig, 1981.

WHYTE, JON: "Mind Over Mountains" in *Mind Over Mountains*. Calgary: Red Deer Press, 2000. "Wenkchemna" in *The Fells of Brightness: Second Volume: Wenkchemna*. Edmonton: Longspoon Press, 1985.

WILSON, SHERI-D: "He Went by Joe" in *The Sweet Taste of Lightning*. Vancouver: Arsenal Pulp Press, 1998.

WIESENTHAL, CHRISTINE: "Avian specimen" in *Instruments of Surrender*. Ottawa: Buschek Books, 2001. Used with permission of Buschek Books.

WISEMAN, CHRISTOPHER: "Calgary 2 A.M." in *An Ocean of Whispers*. Victoria: Sono Nis Press, 1982. "In the Banff Springs Hotel" in *Post-Cards Home: Poems New and Selected*. Victoria: Sono Nis Press, 1988.

WOLFER, STACIE: "Lethbridge" in *Whetstone*, Fall 1994.

WONG, RITA: "Sunset Grocery" in *monkeypuzzle*. Vancouver: Press Gang Publishers, 1998.

WOOLLATT, RICHARD: "Highway 9, East of Hanna," "North & West" & "Roads to Buffalo Lake" in *Eastbound from Alberta*. Red Deer: rdc press, 1981. "North of Three Hills, the Parklands Begin" in *The Prairie Journal of Canadian Literature*, 7 (1986).

ZWICKY, JAN: "Highway 879" in *Songs for Relinquishing the Earth*. London, Ontario: Brick Books, 1998. "Passing Sangudo" in *15 Canadian Poets × 3*, Gary Geddes, ed. Toronto: Oxford University Press, 2001.